COOKING
for
BEGINNERS

KATE FRYER

HarperCollins*Publishers*

Created and produced by
CARROLL & BROWN LIMITED
5 Lonsdale Road
London NW6 6RA

PUBLISHING DIRECTOR Denis Kennedy
ART DIRECTOR Chrissie Lloyd

EDITOR Madeline Weston

DESIGNER Karen Sawyer

PHOTOGRAPHY David Murray, Jules Selmes

FOOD STYLIST Maddalena Bastianelli

PRODUCTION Christine Corton, Wendy Rogers

First published in 1997 by
HarperCollins*Publishers*
77-85 Fulham Palace Road
London W6 8JB

A CIP catalogue record for this book is available from the British Library
ISBN 0 00 414022 2
Printed in Singapore by Tien Wah Press.

CONTENTS

FOREWORD

For those who have never prepared food before, the thought of cooking a meal can be a daunting prospect. What I have tried to do with this book is put together a selection of tasty recipes that are easy to recreate but also will equip the beginner with basic cooking skills. Cooking for Beginners *is intended to build your cooking confidence, and as you master the recipes and techniques in the book, you will feel more at ease preparing food for yourself and your friends.*

I am often told by young friends and acquaintances about their fear, and sometimes dislike, of cooking. Because I like cooking so much myself, I welcome this opportunity to share my enthusiasm with others. To enjoy the preparation of food will make cooking for others a truly pleasurable experience and I hope this book will convince you that you don't have to slave away for hours in the kitchen to produce a delicious meal. The wide range of ready-prepared foods can be combined very successfully with fresh ingredients, to save you time and effort. Cooking for Beginners *is designed to stand on the work area, on view as you prepare and cook the recipe, guiding you through every step. Each recipe is complete on the page, so keeping track of the stages is easy and no page turning is required, leaving your hands free to complete each task. You'll also find a picture of the finished dish with serving suggestions.*

It has been an enjoyable challenge compiling these recipes. I hope when you try them, you find cooking is not as daunting as you thought, and you quickly acquire the skills needed to become more adventurous in the future. Most importantly, however, I hope you relish eating the fruits of your labours!

Kate Fryer

HOW TO USE THIS BOOK

Each of the recipes in this book has been carefully developed to inspire and encourage you to cook, and tested to ensure it's as trouble-free as possible. To be sure of success, it is important to follow the recipe as closely as possible the first time you make it. Once familiar with the steps involved, you can adapt and experiment for yourself.

BEFORE YOU BEGIN

- Read carefully through the recipe you want to cook – you may need to read it twice – but make sure you are familiar with the ingredients required and have the necessary time available.
- Check what ingredients you have to hand and make a comprehensive list of all those you need to buy. Make sure you have the right equipment before you start.
- Collect all the ingredients and equipment together before you begin.
- Weigh and measure the ingredients as necessary (for how to measure accurately, see page 6). All ingredients and equipment are listed in the order they are used.
- For a baked, roasted or grilled dish, it will be necessary to preheat the oven or grill before starting to cook. Check your recipe and, if necessary, switch on the oven at the stated temperature at least 15 mins before you start to cook. Grilling always takes place under a hot grill with the food positioned 5–7.5cm away from the source of heat.

DURING COOKING

- Always wear an apron when you prepare food – this protects the food as well as your clothes!
- Follow the steps in the order they are given. Check the photograph to ensure what you are preparing is what's shown in the picture. As a reminder, the ingredients are repeated in the steps.
- Get into the habit of timing your cooking carefully: using a kitchen timer is the easiest and most exact – if you forget something is cooking you may regret it!
- Follow instructions accurately; for example, do not boil food when simmering is called for in the recipe – it may be spoiled (see page 8).
- Adhere to the rules of food hygiene while preparing food (see page 9).
- When using foil, bear in mind that the shiny side will reflect heat and the dull side will absorb heat. So when lining a grill pan to toast nuts or bread, have the shiny side uppermost; when covering a roasting tin for oven cooking, make sure the dull side is showing.
- Look back at the picture of the finished dish for ideas about presentation and serving suggestions.

NUTRITIONAL INFORMATION

The information indicates nutritional values of the finished dish, but note that extra salt and pepper to taste have not been included in the calculation, as the amount added varies from person to person. Where two alternatives are given, e.g. serves 4 as a main meal, 6 as a starter, nutritional information is based on the first alternative.

EQUIPMENT KNOW-HOW

The recipes in Cooking for Beginners *were designed to require the least amount of equipment possible. In time, as your confidence and cooking ability increases, you will probably want to invest in extra tools and cookware.*

The equipment you buy should be the best you can afford – it will be more reliable to use and last longer. Poorly made equipment is likely to be flimsy and will break or buckle easily, causing you disappointment and frustration!

MEASURING EQUIPMENT

Weighing ingredients accurately is vital to the success of a recipe. Choose a good set of scales with clear numbering (it is helpful to have both metric and imperial measures) and a good size bowl for measuring larger quantities. Liquids are best measured in a jug – a glass one is easiest to read. Ordinary teaspoons and tablespoons vary considerably in size so it is important to invest in a set of metal or plastic spoon measures. They are available from ¼ teaspoon size and will ensure consistent and accurate measuring of small quantities of dry and liquid ingredients.

Liquid measures, such as oil, find their own level but dry ingredients, like baking powder and spices, must be levelled for the measurement to be accurate.

HOW TO MEASURE A LEVEL SPOON
Make sure the spoon measure is full. Hold the spoon over a bowl (or the original container if suitable) to catch the excess. Place the straight edge of a knife blade across the spoon at the handle end. Push the knife away from you, over the spoon to level the surface.

HOW TO CHECK A LIQUID MEASURE
It is important to check liquid measures from eye level, as looking down on the jug will give a distorted view. Stand the jug on a flat surface and wait for the liquid to stop moving. Look at the jug at eye level to check the measurement, the liquid should be exactly on the volume line required.

HOW TO MEASURE THE VOLUME OF EQUIPMENT
A dish or pot should be the correct size for the recipe you are to cook. The most accurate way to measure it is to fill it with water from a measuring jug, rather than the other way round. Using 500ml of cold water at a time, fill the dish until the water reaches the brim, taking note each time you fill the jug.

6

KNIVES

There are lots of different knives for different jobs but for most cutting techniques you will need just three – a large chopping knife and a medium and small all-purpose knife. The size of knife you use should be appropriate to the ingredient you are preparing, and the technique you are performing.

Make sure knives are always sharp to make slicing and chopping more efficient and to prevent accidents – a blunt knife will be less accurate and is more likely to slip. Ideally the blade should be made of stainless steel, with part of the blade extending right to the end of the handle, which should be rivetted together. Hold knives before you buy them. This is the best way to check that the grip is comfortable and that they feel well balanced.

Diced

HOW TO HOLD A KNIFE FOR CHOPPING
A large knife is more efficient when finely chopping herbs or nuts. Hold the tip of the knife firmly to the board, raise and lower the handle working the blade over the food.

Roughly chopped   Finely chopped

CAKE TINS

When checking the size of cake tins, it is the base measurement that gives the actual size of the tin. Check this carefully before using the tin – too large and the cake will be overcooked, too small and it will be under-cooked.

Metal cake tins, with or without a non-stick coating, must be greased to prevent the mixture sticking. Whether you use butter, margarine, white fat or a vegetable oil – only apply a thin but even layer to the inside of the tin. Butter will be easier to spread if used at room temperature.

Sponge and fruit cakes are easier to turn out when their tins are lined (see page 88); however, this is not necessary when cakes or biscuits, such as brownies, have a high fat content. Baking parchment can be used for lining and requires no greasing, but it is quite expensive. Greaseproof paper is a cheaper alternative, but once in the tin the top of the paper must be greased again.

HOW TO MEASURE A CAKE TIN
Turn the tin over, so the flat base is uppermost. Place a ruler across the base to check the size.

HOW TO GREASE A CAKE TIN
Using a piece of kitchen paper, spread the butter over the inside of the cake tin making sure the corners, base and sides are evenly coated.

STOVE TOP PANS AND OVEN DISHES

All stove pans conduct heat through their base. Therefore, bases must be sufficiently thick to ensure maximum efficiency and durability. A ground base on a stainless steel pan is possibly the best quality, but fairly expensive. Oven dishes are often brought from the oven to the table, and can be coloured or decorated, as well as functional.

SAUCEPANS

These should be solidly made and have well fitting lids and heat resistant handles that are securely fixed. Metal saucepans are the best conductors of heat and, if they have a heavy base, they can be used on any type of stove.

Although non-stick saucepans prevent sauces or egg-based recipes from sticking, you cannot use metal tools in them as they can easily scratch. The surface also can deteriorate if the pans are used constantly over high heat.

FRYING PANS

A wide, flat bottomed frying pan with deep sloping sides is best for sautéing (quick frying in a little oil) and stir-frying. Choose a metal frying pan with a heavy base, a lid and a heat resistant handle. The latter is important if you have to finish off a recipe under the grill. For omelette pans, see page 20.

WOKS

This Chinese cooking pan is a versatile piece of kitchen equipment that is increasing in popularity. The curved sides are designed primarily for stir-frying, as in Chilli Stir-Fried Beef, and it can also be used for deep frying or boiling. With a domed lid and metal rack, the wok becomes a steamer. Choose a durable wok that will conduct heat evenly – steel and iron are the best. The handle should be securely fixed, and long enough so that your hand is not too near the heat source.

CASSEROLE DISHES

These dishes can be used on top of the stove for initial browning of meat or softening of vegetables, and then be transferred to the oven for more gentle cooking, as in the recipes for Spicy Lamb Tagine and Beef Goulash. They are usually made of enamelled cast iron or ceramic and come with a lid which should fit tightly, to trap in all the moisture. Casseroles are often brought to the table to serve the finished dish. A casserole dish can also double up as an additional saucepan for boiling vegetables.

BAKING DISHES

Generally available in toughened glass, ceramic or earthenware, these dishes also can be used as serving dishes, so they are often decorated. They do not have lids as the food cooked in them is intended to brown on the top, either in the oven or under the grill after baking in the oven. Make sure when choosing one that it has a lipped rim or handle each side of the dish, to make lifting from the oven easier and safer.

BOILING AND SIMMERING

Boiling liquid has reached 100°C (212°F) but cooking at this temperature can cause some foods to spoil. Simmering is more gentle cooking at a slightly lower temperature: turn the heat down from boiling and allow the liquid to simmer without a lid.

Place the saucepan over high heat. When the water is boiling there should be large bubbles continuously rising to the surface.

When a liquid is simmering, the large bubbles are replaced by a stream of small bubbles that are just visible on the surface.

BASIC EQUIPMENT CHECKLIST

Airtight storage containers	Lemon squeezer
Apron	Measuring jug
Baking sheets	Measuring spoons
Bowls, small, medium and large	Omelette pan (18cm)
Can opener	Oven gloves
Carving knife and fork	Ovenproof dishes (1.1 litre and 1.7 litre)
Casserole with lid, large	Palette knives, large and small
Cling film	Pastry brush with nylon bristles
Colander	Roasting pan with rack
Cutting board	Rolling pin
Electric or rotary hand whisk	Round sandwich tin (20.5cm base measurement)
Foil	
Food bags	Sharp knives, small, medium and large
Frying pan with lid	Sieve
Grater with large and small 'teeth'	Square deep cake tin (20.5cm base measurement)
Greaseproof paper	
Saucepans, small, medium and large	Tea towels
Kitchen paper	Vegetable peeler
Kitchen scales	Wire cooling rack
Kitchen scissors	Wooden spoons

HANDY EXTRAS

Balloon whisk	Meat thermometer	Slotted spoon
Fish slice	Oven thermometer	Toothpicks
Fridge thermometer	Piping bag or syringe and nozzles	Vegetable scrubbing brush
Kitchen string		Wok
Kitchen timer	Potato masher	Wooden spatula
Ladle	Rubber spatula	

FOOD HYGIENE

It is important to be aware of some basic rules of food hygiene in order to avoid any contamination by bacteria that may be in your kitchen or in the food itself. Follow the guidelines below:

- Keep your kitchen and all utensils extremely clean.
- Be meticulous about washing your hands before and after handling food.
- Some raw foods contain natural bacteria, such as salmonella in chicken, so it is particularly important to wash your hands and the utensils immediately after handling, and before continuing any further food preparation.
- Keep separate chopping boards for the preparation of raw and cooked ingredients especially when preparing raw meat. Wash after each use.
- Check the 'sell by' date of the food you buy and any other storage recommendations on the label.
- Do not buy food where the seal is broken, or with damaged packaging such as torn plastic wrapping round meat or poultry.
- After buying, make sure that all perishable food is put in the refrigerator as quickly as possible. This is particularly important in hot weather.
- Store refrigerated food in the correct position and at the correct temperature (see page 94).
- Leftover cooked food should only be reheated once. It must be thoroughly reheated to kill any possible bacteria, so check it is very hot before serving.
- Cook meat and poultry at the temperatures given in the recipes.
- Make sure meat and poultry are thoroughly cooked; a meat thermometer offers a double check when testing whether a large joint of meat is cooked (see page 41). Insert the meat thermometer in the thickest part of the meat, and make sure it does not touch the bone, as this would give a false reading.

CREAMY CORN CHOWDER

Try this rich soup for a start to supper or serve as a warming lunch. Instant mashed potato is a quick and easy way to thicken any soup but complements chowder particularly.

SERVING TIP This could serve six as an appetizer soup. Alternatively, with crusty bread, this chowder could make a meal in itself for four.

COOKING KNOW-HOW

How to Trim and Peel an Onion

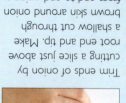

Trim ends of onion by cutting a slice just above root end and tip. Make a shallow cut through brown skin around onion from end to end, using a small sharp knife.

Carefully peel away the thin outer brown skin of the onion and the first layer of the onion flesh using your fingers.

INGREDIENTS

SERVES 6 (OR 4 AS A MAIN COURSE)

50g instant mashed potato	1 medium onion
142ml carton double cream	25g butter
salt and ground black pepper	2 level tsp wholegrain mustard
chopped parsley to garnish	568ml milk
	330g can sweetcorn in water

10

1 Peel 1 onion (see page 10), and cut in half through the core. Dice, by thinly slicing each half lengthwise and then across the slices at right angles.

3 Add 2 tsp mustard to the saucepan and stir well using a wooden spoon. Pour the 568ml milk onto the onion and mustard mixture, stirring continuously. Increase the heat and bring the soup to the boil, stirring continuously.

2 Melt 25g butter in a medium pan until foaming. Add the onion, cover and cook over medium heat for about 10 mins, stirring occasionally.

4 Once the milk mixture has come to the boil, add contents of 330g can sweetcorn with its juice and stir thoroughly with the wooden spoon. Return to the boil, stirring continuously. Then reduce the heat and simmer gently for about 10 mins, stirring occasionally.

5 Sprinkle 50g of instant mashed potato into the saucepan. Stir until well blended and the chowder is thickened slightly, breaking up any lumps with the back of the spoon.

6 Pour in contents of 142ml carton of cream. Continue to cook for 2–3 mins, stirring continuously, until the chowder is smooth and the mashed potato cooked. Add salt and pepper to taste. Take care not to let the soup boil or the cream may curdle and separate. Serve garnished with chopped parsley.

CREAMY CORN CHOWDER (per serving)
- CALORIES 280 • PROTEIN 6g • CARBOHYDRATE 23g
- FAT 19g • CHOLESTEROL 54mg • SODIUM 309mgs

SPICY SQUASH SOUP

Courgettes belong to the squash family of vegetables and for this recipe you can use either green or yellow courgettes. When in season, butternut squash is an excellent alternative. Weigh the butternut before peeling, then peel and cut into 2.5cm dice. If the soup is a too thick, stir in a little water to thin it down. Add the water gradually until you reach the consistency you like.

SERVING TIP

A simple swirl of plain yoghurt or single cream is sufficient garnish for this elegant soup. Drop a spoonful of yoghurt onto the surface of the soup, then draw the tip of the spoon through the centre of the yoghurt to create a swirled effect. Warm naan bread is a good accompaniment. In the summer, this soup is delicious served cold.

INGREDIENTS

SERVES 4

- 1 medium onion
- 900g green or yellow courgettes, washed
- 50g butter
- 1 level tbsp mild curry powder
- 1 level tsp turmeric
- 1 level tsp salt
- ½ level tsp ground ginger
- 600ml water
- ground black pepper
- plain yoghurt or single cream to garnish

SERVE HOT OR COLD

EQUIPMENT • SMALL SHARP KNIFE • CUTTING BOARD • LARGE SAUCEPAN • WOODEN SPOON • SMALL BOWL • MEASURING JUG • LARGE BOWL • SIEVE

1 Peel 1 onion (see page 10) and cut in half through the core. Using a small sharp knife, dice the onion by slicing each half along its length and then across the slices at right angles.

2 Trim 900g courgettes by cutting off about 1cm from the ends. Cut the courgettes crosswise into thick slices.

3 Melt 50g butter in the saucepan until foaming. Add the onion and courgette and stir until coated. Cover; cook over medium heat for 10 mins, stirring occasionally.

6 Stand a large bowl on a damp cloth to steady it. Place a sieve in bowl and pour in the soup a little at a time, pushing it through with the back of the wooden spoon. Rinse out pan; return soup to clean pan, add black pepper to taste and gently reheat. Serve with a swirl of plain yoghurt or single cream.

4 Mix together 1 tbsp curry powder, 1 tsp turmeric, 1 tsp salt and ½ tsp ginger in a small bowl and add to the saucepan. Cook, stirring, for 1 min.

5 Add 600ml water and bring to the boil. Reduce the heat, cover and simmer for about 20 mins or until the vegetables are tender.

SPICY SQUASH SOUP (per serving)
- CALORIES 157 • PROTEIN 5g • CARBOHYDRATE 8g
- FAT 12g • CHOLESTEROL 29mg • SODIUM 606mg

BRUSCHETTA

Loosely translated from Italian, bruschetta means to roast over coals. Ours are simple salsa-topped French bread toasts. Slices of ciabatta work well, too. Without the topping, the bruschetta can be served with a wide range of soups, pastas and salads. Sprinkle them with a little salt and pepper and serve warm.

SERVING TIP
For smaller, party size portions, cut shapes from slices of white or brown bread using pastry cutters, then toast and top with salsa.

INGREDIENTS

SERVES 4

- 1 small French stick
- 1 garlic clove
- 2 tbsp olive oil
- one 225g jar salsa
- basil leaves to garnish

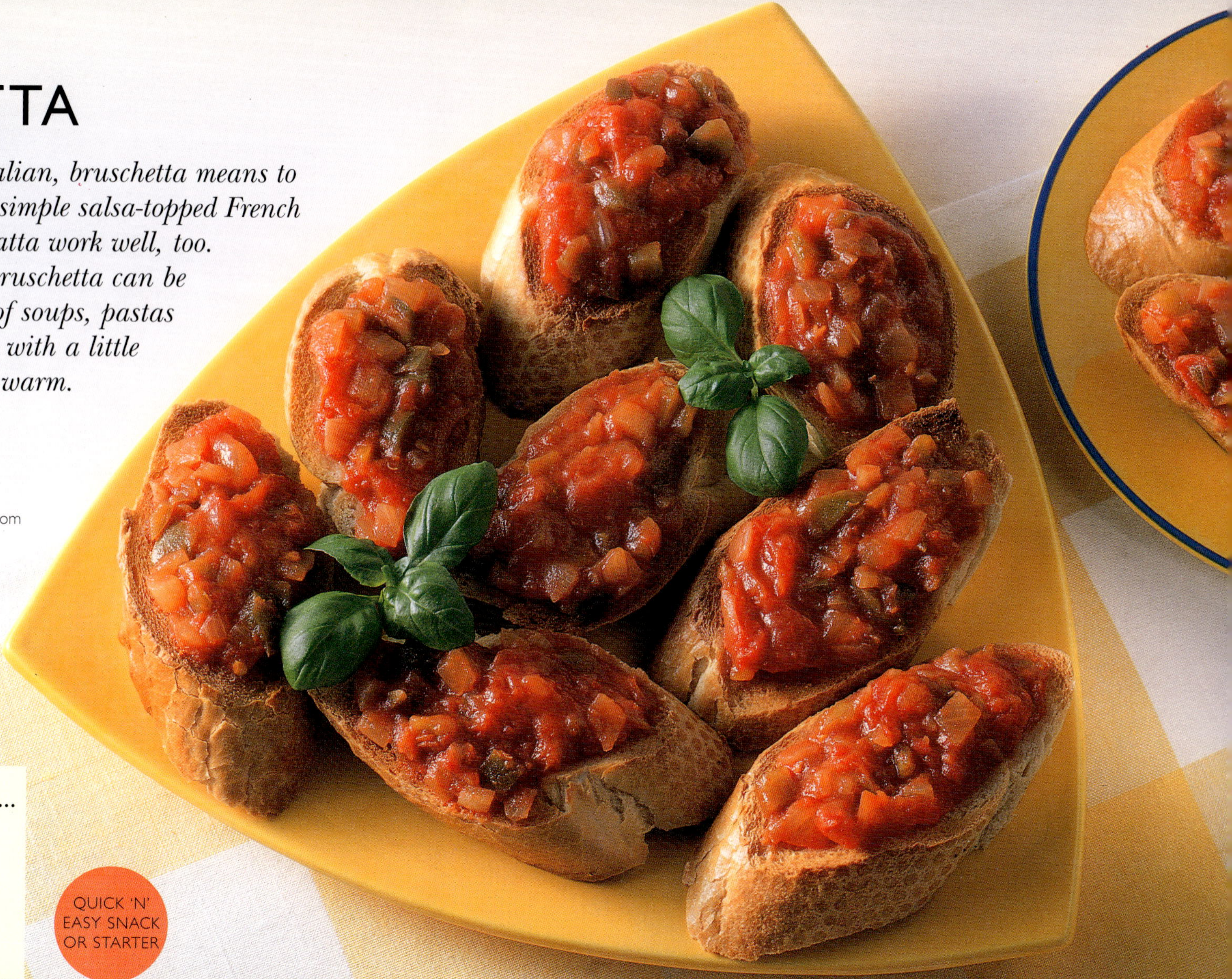

QUICK 'N' EASY SNACK OR STARTER

EQUIPMENT • LARGE SHARP KNIFE • CUTTING BOARD • GRILL PAN AND RACK • SMALL SHARP KNIFE • TEASPOON • SMALL BOWL

1 Trim one end of the French stick diagonally, then slice the loaf into 2.5cm thick diagonal slices.

2 Line grill pan with foil, put bread on grill rack. Place under hot grill and toast about 1 min each side, until golden.

3 With the peel still on the garlic clove, and using a small sharp knife, cut the garlic clove in half lengthwise on the cutting board.

4 Rub the cut edge of each garlic clove half over one side of each warm slice of French bread toast, being careful not to tear toast.

5 Using a teaspoon, carefully drizzle 2 tbsp olive oil evenly over one side of all the toasted bread slices. Work over the grill pan to catch the drips.

6 Spoon a little salsa onto each slice and transfer to serving platter. Garnish with basil leaves and serve at once.

BRUSCHETTA (per serving)
• CALORIES 211 • PROTEIN 6g • CARBOHYDRATE 33g
• FAT 7g • CHOLESTEROL 0mg • SODIUM 853mg

CHICKEN LIVER PÂTÉ

Cooked and chopped up chicken livers form the basis of a tasty starter or sandwich filling. You can use a food processor or blender to purée the livers, but only work them for a very short time or the livers will liquify. Chicken livers should be used as fresh as possible, and cooked quickly – they will become tough with overcooking.

SERVING TIP
Brown or white toast makes an excellent accompaniment for this pâté; serve it as the starter to a special meal with a little salad garnish, or as a quick lunch snack. The pâté is quite rich so a little goes a long way.

INGREDIENTS

SERVES 4

350g chicken livers

125g butter

¼ level tsp dried thyme

150ml orange juice

10 chives

salt and ground black pepper

chives and fresh thyme to garnish

ALLOW FOR CHILLING TIME

EQUIPMENT • COLANDER • KITCHEN SCISSORS • FRYING PAN • WOODEN SPOON • MEASURING JUG • CUTTING BOARD • LARGE SHARP KNIFE • TABLESPOON • 400ML SERVING BOWL

1 Rinse 350g chicken livers in a colander under running cold water and drain well. Trim any white sinew from the livers with kitchen scissors.

2 Melt **about 60g** butter in a frying pan over medium heat until foaming. Add the livers and cook, stirring occasionally, for 3–5 mins.

3 Add ¼ tsp thyme and 150ml orange juice. Snip 10 chives into small pieces and add to pan. Bring to the boil then lower the heat and cook, stirring occasionally, for 8–10 mins, until the liquid is reduced* and the liver cooked.

4 Remove liver mixture from heat and cool for about 10 mins. Add salt and pepper to taste, then turn out onto a cutting board and roughly chop.

5 Spoon the liver mixture into a 400ml serving bowl, pressing it down well with the back of the spoon after each addition so that the mixture is firmly packed.

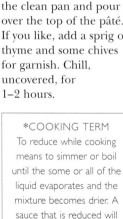

6 Rinse out and dry the frying pan; melt the remaining butter in the clean pan and pour over the top of the pâté. If you like, add a sprig of thyme and some chives for garnish. Chill, uncovered, for 1–2 hours.

*COOKING TERM
To reduce while cooking means to simmer or boil until the some or all of the liquid evaporates and the mixture becomes drier. A sauce that is reduced will become thicker.

CHICKEN LIVER PATE (per serving)
• CALORIES 363 • PROTEIN 17g • CARBOHYDRATE 4g
• FAT 31g • CHOLESTEROL 404mg • SODIUM 313mg

Potato Wedges with Sour Cream Dip

The best potatoes to use for this recipe are the more waxy ones like Cara, Maris Piper and King Edward, which will hold their shapes during roasting.

SERVING TIP
This sour cream dip can also be served with a variety of cocktail biscuits, or with crudités – sticks or pieces of raw seasonal vegetables.

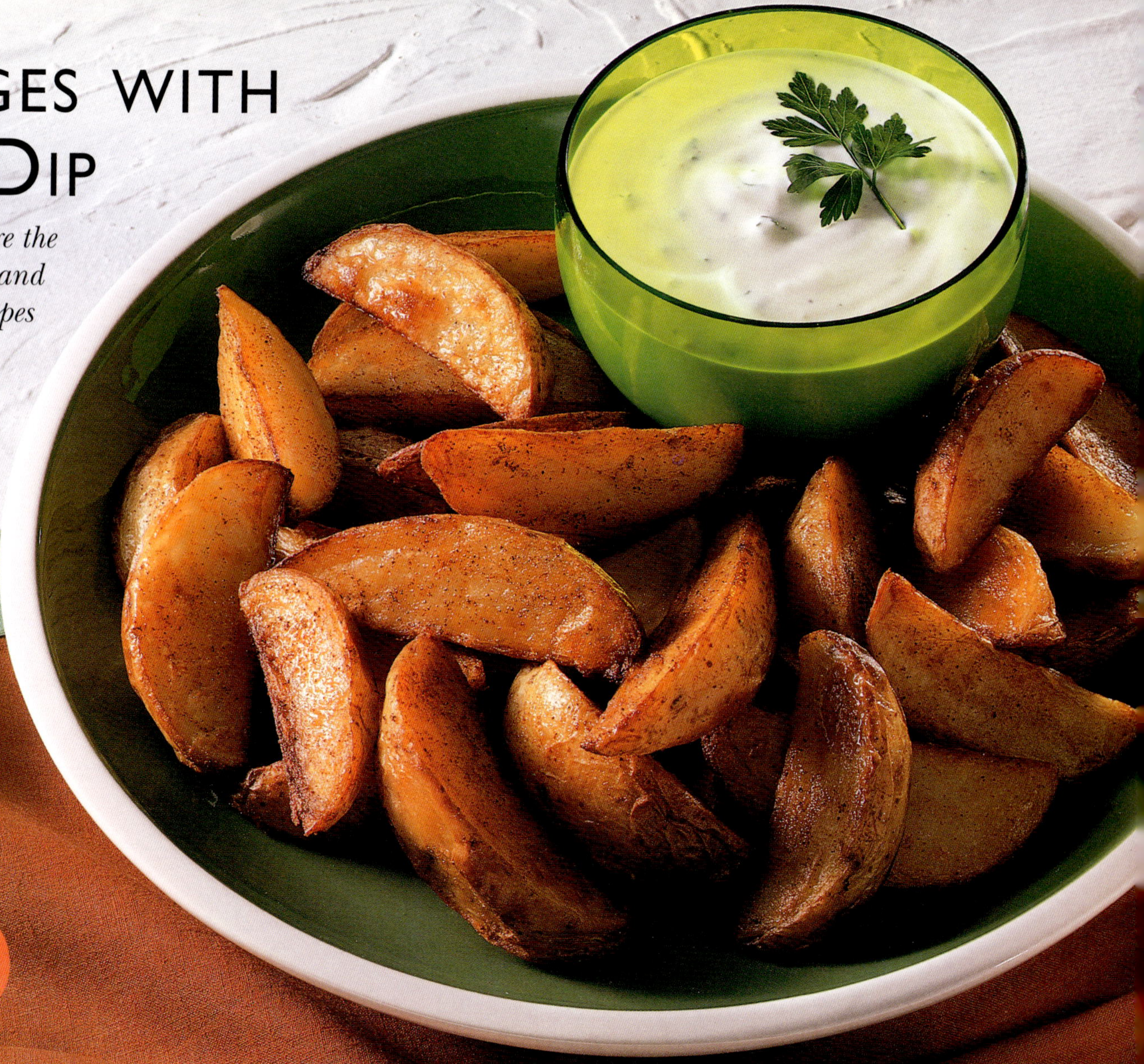

INGREDIENTS

SERVES 4

900g potatoes, washed
1 level tsp salt
1 level tsp paprika
2 tbsp olive oil
4 large sprigs parsley
284ml carton soured cream
ground black pepper
parsley to garnish

SNACK OR SIDE DISH

EQUIPMENT • MEDIUM SAUCEPAN • SMALL SHARP KNIFE • CUTTING BOARD • COLANDER • ROASTING PAN • TABLESPOON • SMALL BOWL • KITCHEN SCISSORS • MEDIUM BOWL

1 Half fill a medium pan with water, cover and bring to the boil. Cut 900g potatoes in half and then each half into even wedges.

2 Add the potato wedges to pan, bring the water back to the boil, reduce the heat and simmer, uncovered, for 5 mins.

3 Drain the potatoes thoroughly through a colander held over the sink, then transfer them to a roasting pan.

4 Sprinkle potatoes with 1 tsp **each** salt and paprika, and drizzle with 2 tbsp olive oil. Toss lightly, then bake in a preheated oven at 200°C (400°F) mark 6 for 30–40 mins or until crisp and golden. Halfway through cooking time, shake pan to prevent sticking.

5 Put 4 large sprigs parsley in a small bowl; snip into small pieces using kitchen scissors.

6 Pour the contents of a 284ml carton soured cream into a medium bowl. Add parsley and black pepper to taste and stir well. Garnish with parsley and serve with the warm potato wedges.

POTATO WEDGES WITH SOUR CREAM DIP (per serving)
- CALORIES 367 • PROTEIN 7g • CARBOHYDRATE 42g
- FAT 20g • CHOLESTEROL 43mg • SODIUM 531mg

CLASSIC OMELETTE

Add variety to this traditional breakfast or light luncheon dish by experimenting with different fillings and flavourings. Chopped tomatoes, mushrooms or cooked chicken can be the starting point for your imagination!

20

INGREDIENTS

SERVES 1 (OR 2 AS A SNACK)

4 eggs, medium

2 tbsp water

salt and ground black pepper

15g butter

COOKING KNOW-HOW

Omelette Pans

• An omelette pan, available in different sizes, is deeper than a frying pan and has curved sides. The best one to buy should have a thick, heavy base and a non-stick finish.

• A heavy based frying pan can be used instead but needs 'seasoning' to keep the egg from sticking.

• To season, sprinkle a little oil and salt over the base and heat slowly until the oil is hot. Remove the pan from the heat, cool slightly and wipe out with a piece of kitchen paper.

A MEAL IN MOMENTS

SERVING TIP

A salad of mixed leaves and cherry tomatoes makes this omelette a complete meal. As an alternative, serve crunchy French bread or oven fried potatoes.

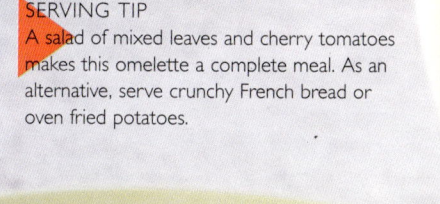

1 Break 4 eggs into a medium bowl, add 2 tbsp water and salt and pepper to taste. Beat the mixture lightly with a fork.

2 Melt 15g butter in an omelette pan until foaming but not beginning to brown. Pour in the beaten egg mixture and tilt the pan slightly so the mixture runs to the sides.

3 Stir with a fork, drawing the set mixture from the sides of the pan into the centre so the uncooked egg can run to the sides.

4 Let cook undisturbed until almost set. The base should be golden and the top still soft. Test by lifting the edge with a palette knife.

5 Tilt the pan away from you and use the palette knife to fold the omelette in half. Let stand for 30 secs to finish cooking the inside. Slide the omelette onto a warm serving plate and serve immediately.

VARIATIONS

CHEESE AND HERB OMELETTE

At the end of Step 1, stir in ½ level tsp dried mixed herbs and 50g grated Cheddar cheese. Complete and serve the omelette following Steps 2 to 5.

SMOKED HAM AND MUSTARD OMELETTE

At the end of Step 1, stir in 1 level tbsp wholegrain mustard. Continue with Steps 2 and 3. At the end of Step 4 sprinkle 25g wafer thin smoked ham over one half of the omelette, then fold and serve the omelette as in Step 5.

CLASSIC OMELETTE (per serving)
• CALORIES 405 • PROTEIN 25g • CARBOHYDRATE 0g
• FAT 34g • CHOLESTEROL 805mg • SODIUM 394mg

FRITTATA

A Mediterranean-style omelette, this contains peppers and Italian sausage which are cooked along with the eggs rather than being folded inside. A frittata is firmer than a French omelette, as it is cooked more slowly. You will find peppered salami at the deli counter in your supermarket but you could substitute any leftover cooked meat or vegetables.

SERVING TIP

Wedges of frittata, whether you serve them warm from the pan or as cold, leftover slices, go well with mixed salad leaves. They are also delicious picnic fare in the summer. Vary the fillings to include mushrooms, tomatoes or sweetcorn.

INGREDIENTS

SERVES 4

1 green pepper
1 red pepper
50g butter
1 tbsp olive oil
75g thinly sliced peppered salami
8 eggs, medium
salt and ground black pepper
125g grated Cheddar cheese

SERVE HOT OR COLD

EQUIPMENT • SMALL SHARP KNIFE • CUTTING BOARD • OVEN-SAFE FRYING PAN • WOODEN SPOON • MEDIUM BOWL • FORK • LARGE PALETTE KNIFE

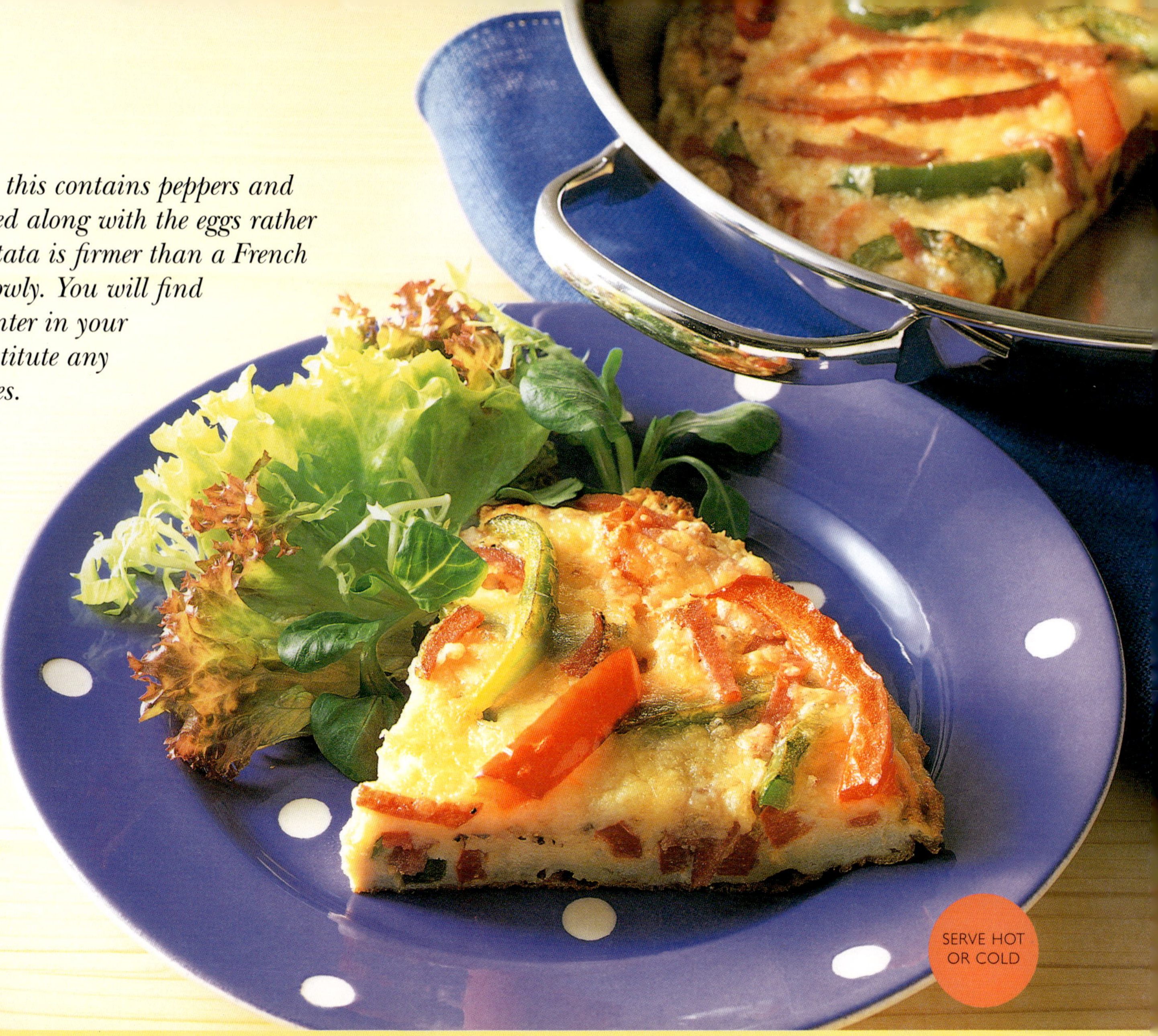

1 Cut 1 red and 1 green pepper in half along their length using a small sharp knife. Remove core, seeds and any white membrane. Cut the flesh of the peppers into finger-length strips.

2 Heat 50g butter and 1 tbsp olive oil in a frying pan until foaming. Add peppers and cook, stirring occasionally, for 8–10 mins or until tender. Stack 75g salami slices in a pile and cut in half. Cut crosswise into fine strips and add to the pan; stir well.

3 With a fork, lightly beat 8 eggs with some salt and pepper. Add to the pan. Stir gently with the wooden spoon to combine the ingredients.

4 Let cook, undisturbed, for 3–5 mins until most of the egg is cooked (set). The base should be golden and the top still soft. Test by lifting the edge with a palette knife.

5 Remove from heat and sprinkle 125g grated cheese on top. Place under a hot grill for 2–3 mins, until bubbling and golden. Cut into wedges and serve.

TECHNIQUE TIP
If your frying pan has a wooden handle, wrap it in foil – shiny side out – to reflect the heat and prevent the wood burning.

FRITTATA (per serving)
- CALORIES 502 • PROTEIN 25g • CARBOHYDRATE 4g
- FAT 43g • CHOLESTEROL 460mg • SODIUM 793mg

PIZZAS

Once you've mastered the techniques of making our quick and easy pizza dough, you'll have the base for an endless number of different toppings, such as sausages, anchovies and ham. Our recipe produces one large or two individual pizza bases. Here it's shown with Two-Cheese topping and you will also find a Pesto, Mushroom and Olive variation.

VARIATION

PESTO, MUSHROOM AND OLIVE PIZZA

SERVES 2

Make the pizza base as in Steps 1 to 5. Instead of the tomato and cheese topping, in Steps 6 and 7, spread **1 level tbsp pesto** evenly over the pizza dough. Drain a **290g jar mushrooms in oil** and spread the mushrooms over the pesto-topped dough. Snip **4 rashers rindless smoked back bacon** into 1cm pieces using kitchen scissors and sprinkle over the mushrooms. Sprinkle the pizza evenly with **2 level tbsp grated Parmesan cheese**, top with **8 pitted black or green olives** and season with **ground black pepper** to taste. Bake in a preheated oven at 200°C (400°F) mark 6 for 15–20 mins.

INGREDIENTS

SERVES 2

For the pizza base:
½ tsp olive oil
1 level tbsp plain flour
145g packet pizza base mix
about 100ml hand-hot water

For the two-cheese topping:
2 level tbsp tomato purée
2 level tsp chilli sauce
75g grated mozzarella cheese
2 fresh plum tomatoes
2 level tbsp grated Parmesan cheese
12 fresh basil leaves
salt and ground black pepper

Two-Cheese Pizza This is a variation on the classic Margherita pizza. Try sun-dried tomatoes for a stronger flavour – and an authentic Italian taste.

ITALIAN FAVOURITE

1 Grease the baking sheet with ½ tsp oil then coat with 1 tbsp flour by tilting and tapping the sides of the baking sheet.

2 Put pizza base mix into a medium bowl. Add about 100ml water a little at a time, stirring with a round-bladed knife to make a soft but not wet dough.

3 Bring the dough together by squeezing it gently with one hand and shaping it into a ball. Lightly flour the work surface, and transfer the dough onto it. Knead gently by pushing the dough away from you with the heel of your hand, then folding it back towards the centre. Turn the dough slightly before kneading again. Continue for about 2 mins until smooth.

4 Turn the dough over; with a rolling pin, roll it into a 23–25.5cm round by working away from you, turning the dough after each rolling movement to keep it in an even shape.

5 Carefully transfer the dough to prepared baking sheet. Pinch the edge of the dough with your thumb and index finger to make a rim. You're now ready to add the topping.

6 In a small bowl, mix 2 tbsp tomato purée and 2 tsp chilli sauce and spread over dough. Sprinkle 75g grated mozzarella on top. Cut 2 tomatoes into thin slices and arrange over the cheese.

7 Sprinkle 2 tbsp Parmesan cheese over the tomato slices and top with 12 basil leaves. Season well with salt and pepper and bake in a preheated oven at 200°C (400°F) mark 6 for 15–20 mins.

TWO-CHEESE PIZZA (per serving)
• CALORIES 637 • PROTEIN 28g • CARBOHYDRATE 97g
• FAT 16g • CHOLESTEROL 81mg • SODIUM 1014mg

GARLIC CHICKEN

A simplified version of the well-known Chicken Kiev, here the home-made butter is spread on top of the chicken rather than placed inside. If garlic isn't to your taste, try the honey and mustard butter variation.

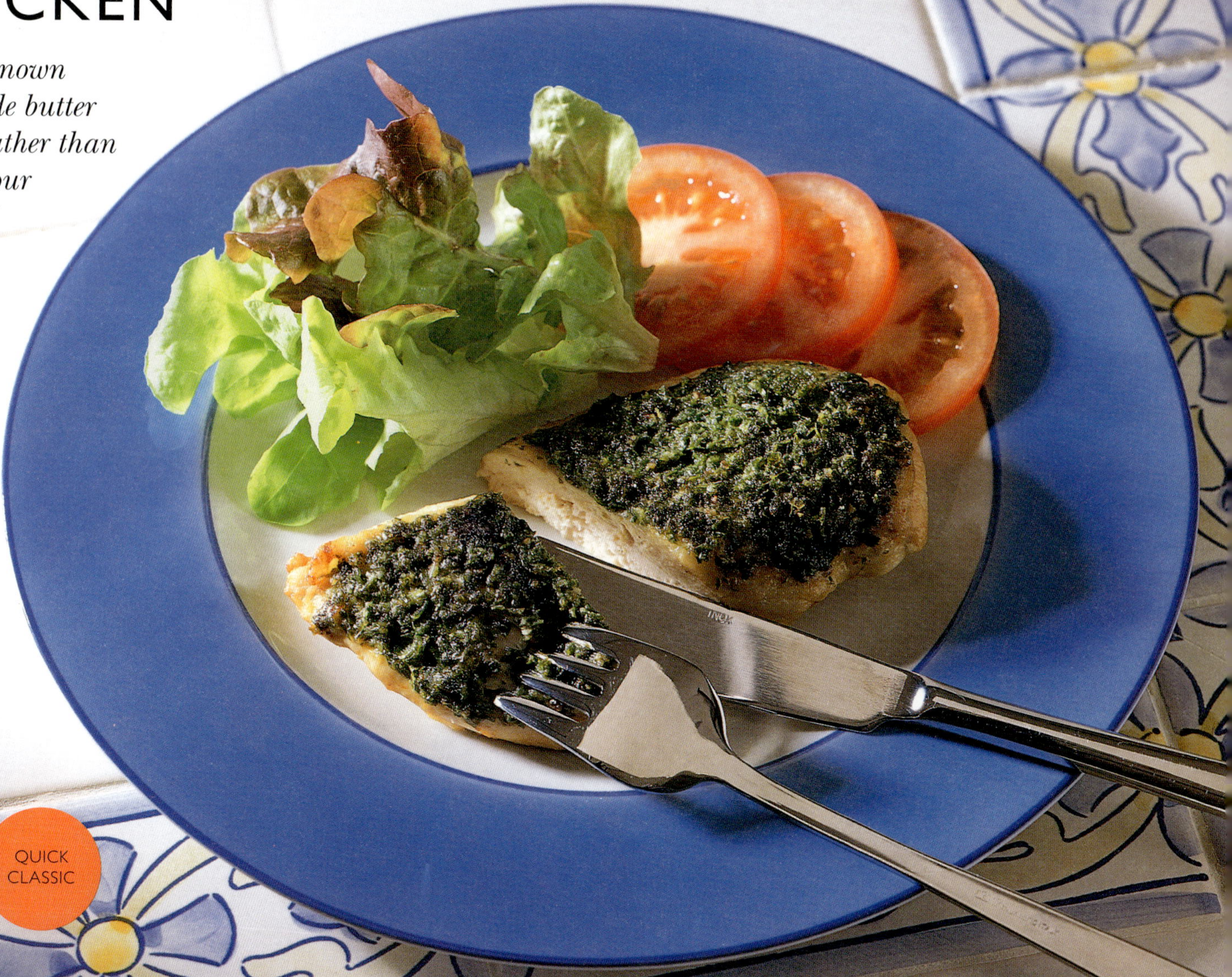

SERVING TIP

A salad makes a refreshing contrast to the richness of the coating on the chicken. For a change, try steamed broccoli florets or carrot sticks.

INGREDIENTS

SERVES 4

- 6 large sprigs parsley
- 75g butter, at room temperature
- 2 level tsp garlic purée
- ground black pepper
- 4 boneless chicken breasts, with skin, about 125g each

QUICK CLASSIC

EQUIPMENT • SMALL BOWL • KITCHEN SCISSORS • MEDIUM BOWL • WOODEN SPOON • SMALL ROASTING PAN • ROUND-BLADED KNIFE • TABLESPOON

1 Put 6 large parsley sprigs in a small bowl, and snip into small pieces using kitchen scissors.

2 Put 75g butter in medium bowl, stand bowl on damp cloth to steady it. Beat butter with wooden spoon until softened.

3 Add the snipped parsley, 2 tsp garlic purée and black pepper to taste to the softened butter, stirring to mix thoroughly.

4 Put 4 chicken breasts, skin side up, in a small roasting pan. Spread the flavoured butter over the skin. Bake in a preheated oven at 200°C (400°F) mark 6 for 10 mins.

VARIATION

HONEY AND MUSTARD CHICKEN

Omit the parsley and garlic purée. In Step 2, beat the butter in a medium bowl until softened. Add **1 level tbsp wholegrain mustard**, **1 level tbsp runny honey**, and **salt and ground black pepper** to taste; beat well until mixed thoroughly. Complete the recipe following Steps 4 and 5.

5 Baste chicken with the flavoured butter and cook for a further 15–20 mins until golden and cooked through: that is, until juices run clear when chicken is pierced with tip of a sharp knife.

GARLIC CHICKEN (per serving)
• CALORIES 429 • PROTEIN 22g • CARBOHYDRATE 0g
• FAT 37g • CHOLESTEROL 167mg • SODIUM 229mg

Chicken Pie

For an elegant looking but easy to make dish, this one is easy as pie. Crunched up filo makes a lighter crust than regular pastry and saves time as well; see below for how to handle the fine sheets. As an alternative topping, use a 400g packet of long-life scalloped potatoes.

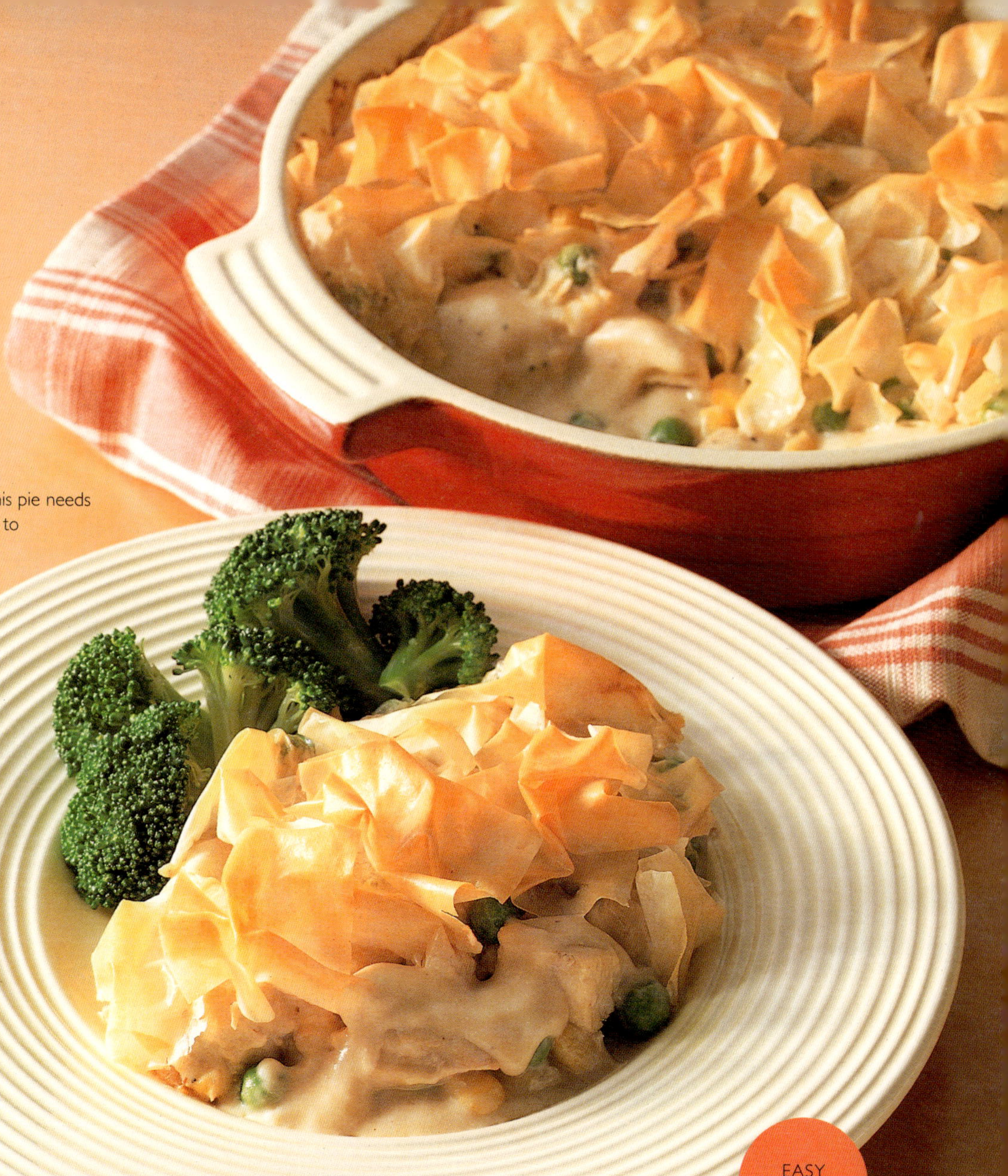

INGREDIENTS

SERVES 4

- 450g boneless, cooked chicken breasts or thighs
- 295g can condensed mushroom soup
- 75g garlic and herb soft cheese
- 150ml milk
- 125g frozen peas
- 125g frozen sweetcorn
- salt and ground black pepper
- 15g butter
- 3 sheets filo pastry

SERVING TIP
Nearly a meal in itself, this pie needs only one fresh vegetable to accompany it – broccoli or carrots are ideal choices.

Cooking Know-how

How to Use Filo Pastry

- Don't let the pastry dry out – keep sheets covered with clingfilm when not in use.
- **Lightly** brush the pastry with melted butter – too much and the pastry will not crisp.
- Any left-over filo can be frozen in handy quantities for another time. Roll in batches of two or three sheets, wrap tightly in cling film, label and freeze.

EASY ELEGANCE

EQUIPMENT • SMALL SHARP KNIFE • CUTTING BOARD • CAN OPENER • MEDIUM SAUCEPAN • WOODEN SPOON • 1.1 LITRE SHALLOW OVENPROOF DISH • SMALL SAUCEPAN • PASTRY BRUSH • CLING FILM

1 Skin 450g chicken breasts or thighs and cut into bite-size pieces.

2 Put contents of 295g can soup, 75g garlic and herb cheese and 150ml milk in a medium saucepan and heat gently, stirring occasionally, until smooth.

3 Stir in the chicken, and 125g **each** peas and sweetcorn. Add salt and pepper to taste and pour into a 1.1 litre shallow ovenproof dish.

6 Lightly scrunch up the pastry pieces and dot over chicken mixture, butter side up. Repeat with remaining sheets of filo to cover the top of the pie. Bake in a preheated oven at 200°C (400°F) mark 6 for 20–30 mins or until golden.

4 Melt 15g butter in a small saucepan and carefully brush a little over the surface of **1 sheet** of filo. Keep the remaining 2 sheets covered with cling film while you are working to prevent them drying out.

5 Using a small sharp knife, cut the buttered filo into squares about 5cm in size. Work carefully to avoid tearing the filo.

CHICKEN PIE (per serving)
• CALORIES 435 • PROTEIN 34g • CARBOHYDRATE 30g
• FAT 21g • CHOLESTEROL 87mg • SODIUM 930mg

Thai Chicken Curry

Thai curries are traditionally served with plenty of boiled rice to absorb all the juices. The coconut milk adds a slightly sweet taste and makes a delicious not-too-hot curry. Most supermarkets now stock a wide range of ethnic ingredients; use either Thai red or green curry paste for this recipe.

SERVING TIP
This curry is full of spice and flavour, so plain rice would be best. For how to cook rice, see page 53. Alternatively, serve it with fine egg noodles.

INGREDIENTS

SERVES 4

175g open mushrooms

6 spring onions

4 skinless, boneless chicken breasts, about 125g each

1 tbsp olive oil

4 level tsp Thai red or green curry paste

150ml water

2 tbsp light soy sauce

400ml can coconut milk

salt and ground black pepper

fresh coriander to garnish

COOKING KNOW-HOW

How to Remove Chicken Fillets

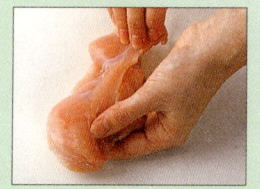

For more even chicken pieces, remove fillet. Pull fillet (the long flap of meat) away from the underside of the chicken breast with your fingers.

EQUIPMENT • KITCHEN PAPER • SMALL SHARP KNIFE • CUTTING BOARD • LARGE FRYING PAN • WOODEN SPOON • MEASURING JUG • CAN OPENER

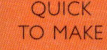

QUICK TO MAKE

1 Wipe 175g open mushrooms clean with damp kitchen paper. Cut each mushroom in half then each half into four.

2 Trim 6 spring onions just above root end then peel away outer layer. Cut off dark green leaves. Cut diagonally into 5mm slices.

3 Using the small sharp knife, and working on the cutting board, cut 4 chicken breasts and fillets into bite-size pieces.

6 Stir in mushrooms, spring onions, and salt and pepper to taste. Simmer for about 8 mins or until the chicken is cooked. Serve garnished with coriander.

4 Heat 1 tbsp oil and 4 tsp curry paste in a large frying pan. Add chicken and cook, stirring, for about 2 mins.

5 Pour in 150ml water, 2 tbsp light soy sauce and contents of 400ml can of coconut milk and bring to the boil, stirring to mix thoroughly.

THAI CHICKEN CURRY (per serving)
• CALORIES 216 • PROTEIN 29g • CARBOHYDRATE 6g
• FAT 8g • CHOLESTEROL 54mg • SODIUM 280mg

BARBECUE SPARE RIBS

These ribs are very easy to make so don't be put off by the long cooking time; they don't need much watching so you can entertain your guests while they cook. Remember to supply everyone with lots of paper napkins and a bowl of warm water for their fingers.

SERVING TIP
Radishes make a crunchy garnish to a spare ribs starter. For a main meal, baked potatoes would go perfectly with the barbecued ribs. Bake the potatoes alongside the ribs in the oven (see page 65).

32

INGREDIENTS
....
SERVES 2 (OR 4 AS A STARTER)

2 level tsp garlic purée

1 level tbsp chilli sauce

3 tbsp barbecue sauce

2 tbsp dark soy sauce

3 level tbsp tomato ketchup

230g can chopped tomatoes

50ml white wine vinegar

50g soft light brown sugar

salt and ground black pepper

1kg pork spare ribs

radishes to garnish

MAIN COURSE OR STARTER

STICKY CHOCOLATE BROWNIES (per serving)
• CALORIES 464 • PROTEIN 6g • CARBOHYDRATE 44g • FAT 31g • CHOLESTEROL 70mg • SODIUM 216mg

1 Grease a 20.5cm base measurement, square deep cake tin (see page 7). Break 225g white chocolate onto a cutting board and roughly chop. Hold tip of knife firmly to the board, raise and lower handle working the blade over the chocolate.

2 Break 350g chocolate into a medium bowl, and add 225g butter. Place over a small saucepan of simmering water (see page 74). Beat with a wooden spoon when melted.

3 Remove the bowl from the pan of hot water and allow to cool slightly. In a large bowl mix together 3 eggs, 3 tbsp honey and 225g soft light brown sugar, then gradually beat in the melted chocolate mixture with the wooden spoon until thoroughly combined.

4 Add 75g self-raising flour, ¼ tsp salt, 175g walnut pieces and chopped white chocolate to the bowl. Gently fold the ingredients together using a tablespoon. Pour the mixture into the prepared tin.

5 Gently tap the tin on the counter to level the surface; stand it on a baking sheet and bake in a preheated oven at 170°C (325°F) mark 3 for 30 mins then cover loosely with foil. Bake for a further 45 mins. The centre should be a little soft. Cool in the tin.

6 When cold, tip the cake onto a board, turn it over, and trim the edges using a large sharp knife. Cut into about 16 squares.

Store Cupboard

If you have bread, potatoes, onions, flour, sugar, eggs, butter, oil and cheese, you can always whip up something tasty and never go hungry!

The storecupboard, moreover, can also be a source of inspiration if kept well stocked. There are now so many different ingredients to choose from, it is often difficult to know which ones to buy. Begin by buying the basics then build up your stocks gradually, acquiring ingredients as you need them.

STORECUPBOARD ITEMS

Biscuits, such as digestives and ratafias	Jars of Oriental and Indian curry pastes
Canned coconut milk	Mayonnaise
Canned chopped tomatoes	Olive and vegetable oil
Canned fruit	Packets of dried pasta
Canned kidney or cannellini beans	Packets of long-life potatoes
Canned tuna	Potato crisps
Chilli sauce	Rice
Dried fruit	Soy sauce
Dried herbs and spices	Stock cubes
Flour tortillas	Sugar
Garlic purée	Tomato ketchup
Instant noodles	Tomato purée
Jar of pasta sauce	White wine vinegar
Jars of marmalade, lemon curd and jam	Wholegrain mustard
	Worcestershire sauce

STORAGE TIPS

- Most jars once opened will keep well in the store cupboard; however, some will last longer if kept in the refrigerator, so check the label.
- Dry stores like pasta, rice and sugar should be transferred to airtight containers or tied into food bags for continued storage.
- Label the jar or bag with the date you opened it.
- Stack newly bought items behind opened packets of the same ingredient so you use them in order of date of purchase.

SUBSTITUTIONS

You may not always have exactly the right ingredients to hand so substituting or doubling up one or two ingredients may be the answer. If, for example, the recipe calls for a herb you don't have or like, use parsley instead; and if you don't have fresh herbs then use **half** the quantity of dried. Other easy substitutions would be using canned salmon instead of tuna, raisins instead of sultanas, or milk chocolate instead of plain. You can substitute a different kind of nut for the ones used in a recipe; walnuts, hazelnuts, almonds and pecans are all interchangeable but the taste will be slightly different.

REFRIGERATOR FACTS

- For safe food hygiene, use a fridge thermometer and keep your refrigerator at a temperature of between 1°C (35°F) and 5°C (40°F).
- The most important thing to remember is to keep raw and cooked foods, particularly meats, separate from each other.
- Store raw meat, covered, in the bottom of the refrigerator to prevent raw meat juices dripping onto other foods.
- Cover all food that is stored in the refrigerator to prevent it drying out and to prevent strong flavoured foods from tainting others.
- Make sure any hot food has cooled to room temperature before covering and putting in the refrigerator.

FREEZER FACTS

- Before buying frozen foods double check the star rating of your freezer – this will give you a guide as to how long you can store foods: * up to 1 week, ** up to 1 month, *** up to 3 months.
- There are a few useful items that are worth keeping in the freezer if you have space: frozen vegetables and potato products, bread, packets of filo and shortcrust pastry, ice cream and herbs.
- Make sure that any hot food is cooled to at least room temperature before freezing.
- Make sure you identify all foods by labelling and dating them – it is very easy to forget what you have in the freezer!
- The safest way to thaw frozen food is in the refrigerator overnight. However, check the packaging of ready-prepared foods, as many of them are cooked from frozen.

1 Put all the ingredients, except the spare ribs, into a large bowl and mix thoroughly with a spoon.

2 Add 1kg spare ribs and coat thoroughly with sauce. Cover with cling film and let marinate* in the refrigerator for 30 mins.

3 Pour the spare ribs and the sauce into a large roasting pan, making sure the ribs are in a single layer to ensure even cooking.

4 Cover tightly with foil, dull side out, by turning the foil under the rim of the pan; bake in a preheated oven at 190°C (375°F) mark 5 for 1 hour.

5 Remove foil from the roasting pan and baste the spare ribs with the sauce. Bake, uncovered, for about 30 mins longer until tender and cooked through. Baste again, and serve piled on a platter garnished with radishes.

*COOKING TERM
To marinate means to soak in a liquid flavoured with herbs and seasonings. This both flavours and tenderizes the meat. Cover and refrigerate meat when it is in the marinade.

BARBECUE SPARE RIBS (per serving)
• CALORIES 1157 • PROTEIN 65g • CARBOHYDRATE 41g
• FAT 82g • CHOLESTEROL 248mg • SODIUM 746mg

PORK WITH APPLE AND SAGE

HEARTY
MAIN DISH

*The complementary flavours of apple and pork combine
perfectly in this delicious and substantial dish. Pork
should be well cooked: pierce the chops with the
tip of a sharp knife and see that the juices
run clear. This recipe also works well
with skinless, boneless chicken
breasts or turkey steaks; check
they are done by testing
in the same way.*

SERVING TIP
Accompany with creamy mashed potatoes to
soak up the delicious sauce. For a special
occasion, use cider in place of the apple juice
to make the dish even more flavourful.

34

INGREDIENTS

SERVES 2

1 tbsp olive oil

2 rindless, bone-in pork loin chops,
about 175g each

½ level tsp dried sage

salt and ground black pepper

150ml apple juice

6 spring onions

1 red skinned eating apple

4 level tbsp crème fraîche

EQUIPMENT • FRYING PAN WITH LID • LARGE PALETTE KNIFE • FORK • MEASURING JUG • SMALL SHARP KNIFE • CUTTING BOARD • WOODEN SPOON • TABLESPOON

1 Heat 1 tbsp oil in large frying pan. Add 2 pork chops and cook 1–2 mins each side to brown and seal.

2 Add ½ tsp sage, salt and pepper to taste and 150ml apple juice. Bring to the boil, cover and simmer for about 8 mins.

3 Meanwhile, trim 6 spring onions just above root end. Peel outer layer and cut off dark green leaves. Cut diagonally into 5mm slices.

4 Cut 1 eating apple in half through core. Cut each piece in half, remove core and thickly slice the flesh along its length.

5 Stir in the apple and spring onions. Simmer, uncovered, for 3–5 mins. Apple slices should be cooked but retain their shape, and the pork well done.

6 Stir in 4 tbsp crème fraîche and heat gently for 1 min longer, stirring to mix with the juices. Take care not to let the sauce boil or the crème fraîche may curdle.

PORK WITH APPLE AND SAGE (per serving)
• CALORIES 691 • PROTEIN 25g • CARBOHYDRATE 17g
• FAT 58g • CHOLESTEROL 137mg • SODIUM 98mg

Lamb Kofta Kebabs

The coriander and cumin used to flavour the meat, and the fresh cucumber raita, give an authentic Middle Eastern taste to the kebabs. As well as a main meal, these kebabs could also be served as a starter, or as party fare.

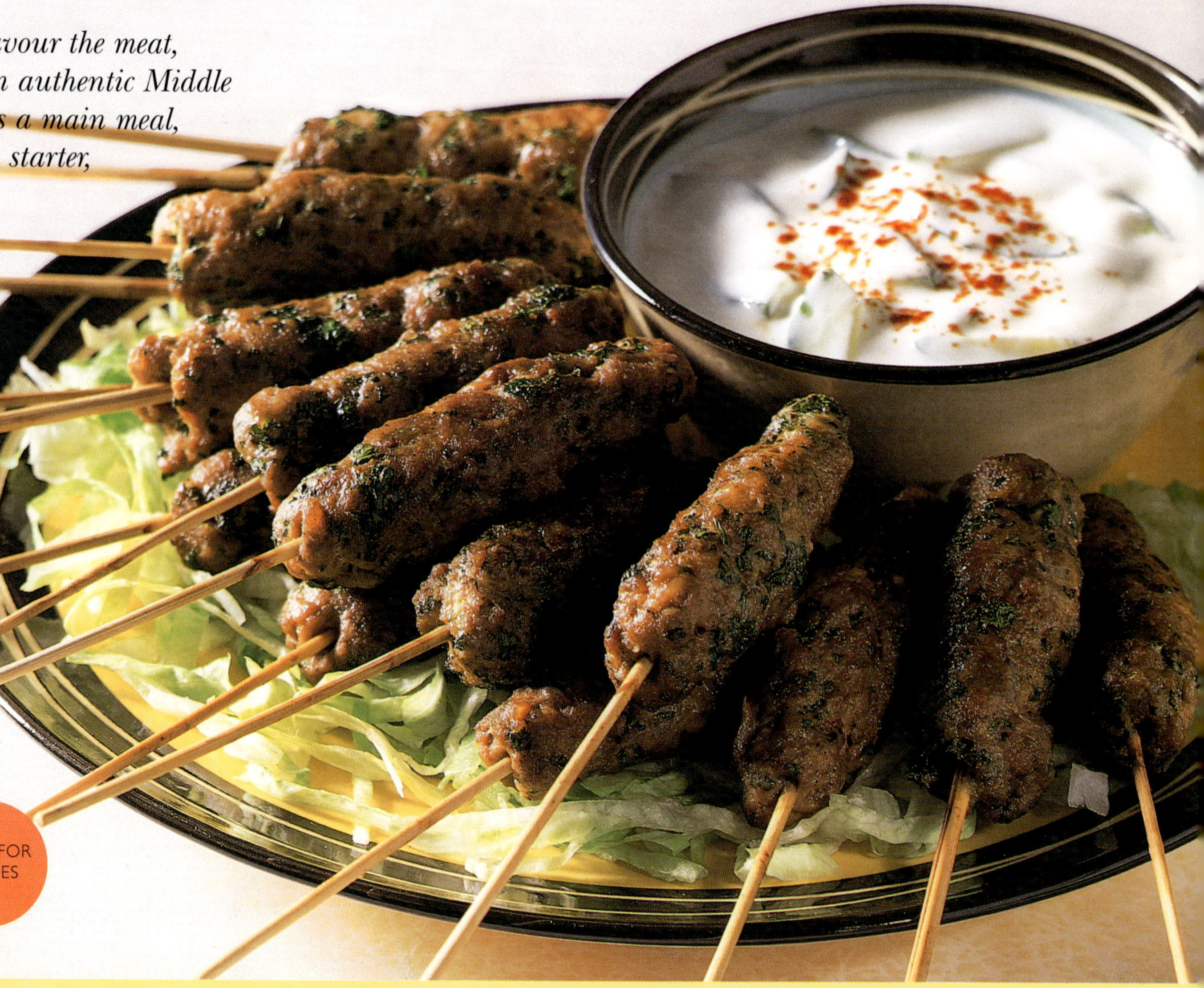

SERVING TIP

Place the kebabs on a bed of shredded lettuce, with the cucumber raita on the side. As an alternative, shape the meat mixture into 8 burgers, grill and serve in sesame buns with tomato slices and relish.

INGREDIENTS

SERVES 4 (OR 8 AS A STARTER)

8 stalks fresh coriander
8 sprigs parsley
1 slice white bread, crusts removed
3 tbsp milk
450g minced lamb
1 level tbsp ground cumin
½ level tsp salt
½ level tsp ground black pepper
1 level tsp garlic purée
125g piece cucumber
two 142ml cartons natural yogurt
paprika to garnish

IDEAL FOR PARTIES

EQUIPMENT • LARGE SHARP KNIFE • CUTTING BOARD • 16 WOODEN SATAY STICKS ABOUT 15CM • LARGE PLATE • SMALL PLATE • LARGE BOWL • WOODEN SPOON • GRILL PAN WITH RACK • FOIL • SMALL SHARP KNIFE • MEDIUM BOWL

1 Cut woody stalks from 8 stalks coriander then chop finely with 8 sprigs of parsley: hold tip of large sharp knife firmly to the board, raise and lower handle, working blade over herbs.

2 Put 16 satay sticks in hot water in large plate and leave to soak. Soak 1 slice of bread in 3 tbsp milk in small plate for 5 mins.

3 Put 450g minced lamb, coriander and parsley, 1 tbsp cumin, ½ tsp **each** salt and pepper, and 1 tsp garlic purée in large bowl. Squeeze milk from bread, add bread to bowl and mix thoroughly. Discard milk.

4 Using **about 2 level tbsp** of meat mixture each time, roll the pieces into even sausage shapes using wet hands, to make 16 in all. Skewer through centres with soaked satay sticks.

5 Put kebabs on grill rack in grill pan lined with foil. Cook under a hot grill for about 8 mins for slightly pink, or 10 mins for well done, turning frequently.

TECHNIQUE TIP
Cover sticks with foil, if necessary, to prevent burning.

6 With small sharp knife, cut 125g cucumber in half along length, then each piece into four. Stand pieces on their ends and cut away seeds; thinly slice crosswise. Pour contents of two 142ml yogurt cartons into a medium bowl, stir in cucumber and salt and pepper to taste. Serve kebabs garnished with paprika.

LAMB KOFTA KEBABS (per serving)
• CALORIES 353 • PROTEIN 26g • CARBOHYDRATE 11g
• FAT 23g • CHOLESTEROL 89mg • SODIUM 403mg

SPICY LAMB TAGINE

Couscous is a traditional accompaniment to spicy meat stews, like this tagine, and is used extensively in North African cuisine. For the best flavour, plan ahead and leave the meat to marinate overnight.

COOKING KNOW-HOW

Couscous

Allow about 50g of couscous per person as a side dish.

- Place the couscous in a large bowl, cover with cold water and leave to soak for about 10 mins.
- Drain through a sieve and tip the soaked grains onto a baking sheet, spreading them out into a thin layer. Allow to dry for about 15 mins.
- Line the sieve with a clean cloth, add the couscous then place the sieve over a pan of boiling water or stock.
- Cover and steam for about 15 mins until the grains are fluffy and warmed through.
- Separate the grains with a fork before serving.

Boil in the bag and flavoured instant varieties are also available. They take much less time to prepare and are convenient to use. Always follow the instructions given on the packet.

SERVING TIP

Couscous is ideal for soaking up the juices in this stew, but for a change try creamy mashed potatoes or rice.

INGREDIENTS

SERVES 4

900g boneless lamb, such as shoulder or chump steaks

1 medium onion

1 level tsp **each** ground cumin, coriander, ginger and dried thyme

2 tbsp olive oil

300ml orange juice

2 level tbsp plain flour

600ml chicken stock

125g no-soak dried apricots

fresh mint to garnish

couscous to serve

PREPARE AT LEAST 5 HOURS AHEAD

EQUIPMENT • SMALL SHARP KNIFE • CUTTING BOARD • LARGE BOWL • LARGE CASSEROLE WITH LID • WOODEN SPOON • SMALL BOWL • TEASPOON

1 Trim fat from 900g lamb, using a small sharp knife, then cut the meat into 2.5cm cubes.

2 Peel 1 onion (see page 10) and cut in half through core. With knife at right angles to core, cut the onion into thin slices.

3 Put the sliced onion, 1 tsp **each** cumin, coriander, ginger and thyme and **1 tbsp** of oil in a large bowl. Add the lamb and stir well. Cover and refrigerate for at least 3 hours or overnight to marinate (see page 33) and allow the meat to absorb the flavours.

4 Heat remaining 1 tbsp oil in large casserole. Add lamb mixture and stir fry by stirring constantly over high heat for about 5 mins until browned, to seal the meat (see page 47).

5 In a small bowl, gradually blend 300ml orange juice into 2 tbsp flour until smooth. Add to casserole with 600ml stock. Bring to the boil, stirring, then cover and cook in a preheated oven at 170°C (325°F) mark 3 for 1 hr.

6 Remove the casserole from oven. Add 125g apricots, stir and cover and return to oven. Cook for about 20 mins or until tender. Garnish with fresh mint and serve with couscous.

SPICY LAMB TAGINE (per serving)
• CALORIES 485 • PROTEIN 43g • CARBOHYDRATE 29g
• FAT 23g • CHOLESTEROL 148mg • SODIUM 368mg

ROAST LEG OF LAMB

A juicy tasty lamb roast makes a delicious substantial lunch or dinner – and is quite easy to cook. Beef and pork can be cooked similarly, see page 41.

SERVING TIP
Roast potatoes are a classic accompaniment. Boil the potatoes as on page 68 for 5 mins and drain. Cook them for about 1 hour in a little hot olive oil in a separate tin above the joint, turning regularly to ensure they are golden brown all over.

COOKING KNOW-HOW

How to Carve a Leg of Lamb

With leg of lamb flat side down on cutting board, cut out a wedge of meat near the narrow end, cutting through to the bone. Remove wedge of meat. Cut thin slices, working back along leg.

Turn the leg of lamb over and steady the meat with the carving fork. Carve long thin slices of meat working towards the fork, parallel to the bone.

INGREDIENTS

SERVES 4

1 garlic clove
1kg leg of lamb
salt and ground black pepper
four 2.5cm sprigs fresh rosemary

SPECIAL LUNCH OR DINNER

EQUIPMENT • SMALL SHARP KNIFE • CUTTING BOARD • ROASTING PAN WITH RACK • TABLESPOON • CARVING KNIFE AND FORK

2 Stand joint on board and season with salt and ground black pepper. Make 8 incisions in the lamb, spacing them well apart. Insert a piece of garlic or sprig of rosemary into each one.

1 Preheat oven to 180°C (350°F) mark 4. Trim end of 1 garlic clove and peel away skin. Cut garlic clove in half along length and then in half again.

3 Stand the joint on a rack in a roasting pan and place in preheated oven for about 1½ hrs for medium and 1¾ hrs for well done.

4 Baste the joint with the pan juices at regular intervals – about every 30 mins. Test the lamb is cooked (see box, right), remove the garlic and rosemary and let the joint stand before carving.

COOKING KNOW-HOW

How to Roast and Carve a Joint of Meat

- Choose a good quality cut that has an even outer layer of fat and some marbling of fat through the meat.
- Allow about 225g of meat per person for a boneless joint and about 275g per person for a bone-in joint.
- Roasting is generally done at 180°C (350°F) mark 4 which will ensure moist meat with little shrinkage.
- Cook beef and lamb to medium for 25 mins per 450g plus 25 mins, and for well done, 30 mins per 450g plus 30 mins. For pork, allow 30 mins per 450g plus 30 mins for medium, and 35 mins per 450g plus 35mins for well done.
- Stand the joint, fat side up, on a rack in the roasting pan. Use the juices that drain from the meat to baste the joint at regular intervals, about every 30 mins.
- To check the meat is cooked, pierce the flesh at the thickest part using a small sharp knife; the juices should run clear. If pink, roast a little longer and test again.
- If you want to invest in a meat thermometer, this is a very accurate way of checking the meat is cooked and eliminates a lot of the guess work. Medium will be 70°C (160°F) and well done, 80°C (180°F).
- Put the cooked joint on a cutting board, cover with a loose tent of foil and leave for about 15 mins to stand. This allows the juices to settle and makes the meat easier to carve.
- Use a long-bladed, sharp carving knife – the blade should extend about 5cm either side of the joint to take into account the sawing action of carving.
- A two-pronged carving fork is important to steady the meat as you carve, and ideally should have a finger guard to give you added protection.
- As a general rule, cut the meat at right angles to the bone, across the grain; this will shorten the fibres making the meat more tender.

ROAST LEG OF LAMB (per serving)
- CALORIES 464 • PROTEIN 35g • CARBOHYDRATE 0g
- FAT 36g • CHOLESTEROL 150mg • SODIUM 100mg

ONE POT
MEAL

CHILLI CON CARNE

This easy dinner dish originated in Texas: its name is Spanish for chilli with meat. Our version is medium-hot and will suit most palates. When cooking for two, it is worth making a full batch of chilli and freezing the rest as the flavours are even better when reheated.

SERVING TIP
If you want to eat your chilli Tex-Mex style, use pieces of the flour tortillas to scoop up mouthfuls of the chilli. This chilli also makes an ideal topping for baked potatoes (see page 65).

INGREDIENTS

SERVES 4

1 medium onion
1 tbsp olive oil
2 level tbsp chilli sauce
1 level tsp garlic purée
700g minced beef
420g can red kidney beans
400g can chopped tomatoes

2 tbsp Worcestershire sauce
2 level tbsp tomato ketchup
1 beef stock cube
salt and ground black pepper
fresh coriander and soured cream to garnish

COOKING KNOW-HOW

How to Warm Flour Tortillas

IN THE OVEN
Wrap up to 8 tortillas in foil and place in a preheated oven at 170°C (325°F) mark 3 for about 15 minutes.

UNDER A GRILL
Place two tortillas at a time under a hot grill, and heat for 8–10 seconds each side.

IN A MICROWAVE
Stack up to 8 tortillas on a plate, cover loosely with clingfilm and microwave on full power for 40–60 seconds; for single tortillas, 8–10 seconds, for a 700 watt microwave, or check your microwave handbook.

Serve the warmed tortillas immediately – keep them warm by wrapping in foil or a napkin.

1 Peel 1 onion (see page 10) and cut in half through core. Dice by slicing each half along its length and then across the slices at right angles.

2 Heat 1 tbsp oil in large saucepan. Add onion and cook, stirring occasionally, for about 5 mins.

3 Add 2 tbsp chilli sauce, 1 tsp garlic purée and 700g minced beef. Cook, stirring constantly, for about 3 mins until the meat browns.

4 Drain 420g can of kidney beans in a colander and rinse under cold running water.

5 Add contents of 400g can of chopped tomatoes, 2 tbsp Worcestershire sauce, 2 tbsp tomato ketchup and the kidney beans to saucepan and stir well. Bring to the boil, reduce heat, cover and simmer for about 30 mins, stirring occasionally.

6 Crumble 1 stock cube into chilli, add salt and pepper to taste and stir well. Simmer, uncovered, for about 10 mins. Garnish with coriander and soured cream. Serve with tortillas.

CHILLI CON CARNE (per serving)
- CALORIES 518 • PROTEIN 39g • CARBOHYDRATE 20g
- FAT 32g • CHOLESTEROL 116mg • SODIUM 536mg

CHILLI STIR-FRIED BEEF

Chilli peppers are used as an ingredient in the cuisines of countries all over the world, but they are difficult to prepare fresh. Chilli powder is made of dried chillies and gives you all the taste without the tiresome preparation. If you like very spicy food, double the quantity of chilli powder!

SERVING TIP
To make a chilli flower, make two or three cuts along the length of a small red chilli, starting just above the stalk and turning between each cut. Place in a bowl of iced water for about 1 hour to make it curl like flower petals.

INGREDIENTS

SERVES 4
700g rump steak

1 level tsp **each** ground ginger, salt, ground black pepper, ground cumin and chilli powder

1 level tbsp dark brown sugar

8 spring onions

1 tbsp olive oil

2 tbsp lemon juice

100ml water

instant egg noodles to serve

chilli flowers to garnish

EQUIPMENT • LARGE SHARP KNIFE • CUTTING BOARD • LARGE FOOD BAG • SMALL SHARP KNIFE • FRYING PAN • WOODEN SPOON • MEASURING JUG

DINNER PARTY DISH

1 With a large sharp knife, cut away any fat from 700g rump steak then slice the beef across the grain, into wafer-thin strips.

2 Put the spices and 1 tbsp sugar into large food bag. Add beef; twist top of bag and shake to coat.

3 Trim 8 spring onions just above root with a small sharp knife; peel away outer layer. Cut off dark green leaves.

4 Cut the trimmed spring onions across diagonally, into 5mm slices.

6 Add 2 tbsp lemon juice and 100ml water. Cook for about 5 mins, stirring often, until the beef is cooked and the sauce reduced (see page 17). Serve with instant egg noodles, garnished with reserved spring onions and chilli flowers.

5 Heat 1 tbsp olive oil in frying pan until very hot. Add **half** the spring onions and all the sliced beef, separating the slices with your fingers. Stir fry by stirring constantly over high heat for 2 mins.

CHILLI STIR-FRIED BEEF (per serving)
• CALORIES 247 • PROTEIN 32g • CARBOHYDRATE 6g
• FAT 10g • CHOLESTEROL 91mg • SODIUM 595mg

Beef Goulash

Paprika is made of ground sweet red peppers which are related to chillies but do not have the fiery taste; it is popular in Hungarian cuisine where it is used to add flavour and aroma as well as colour.

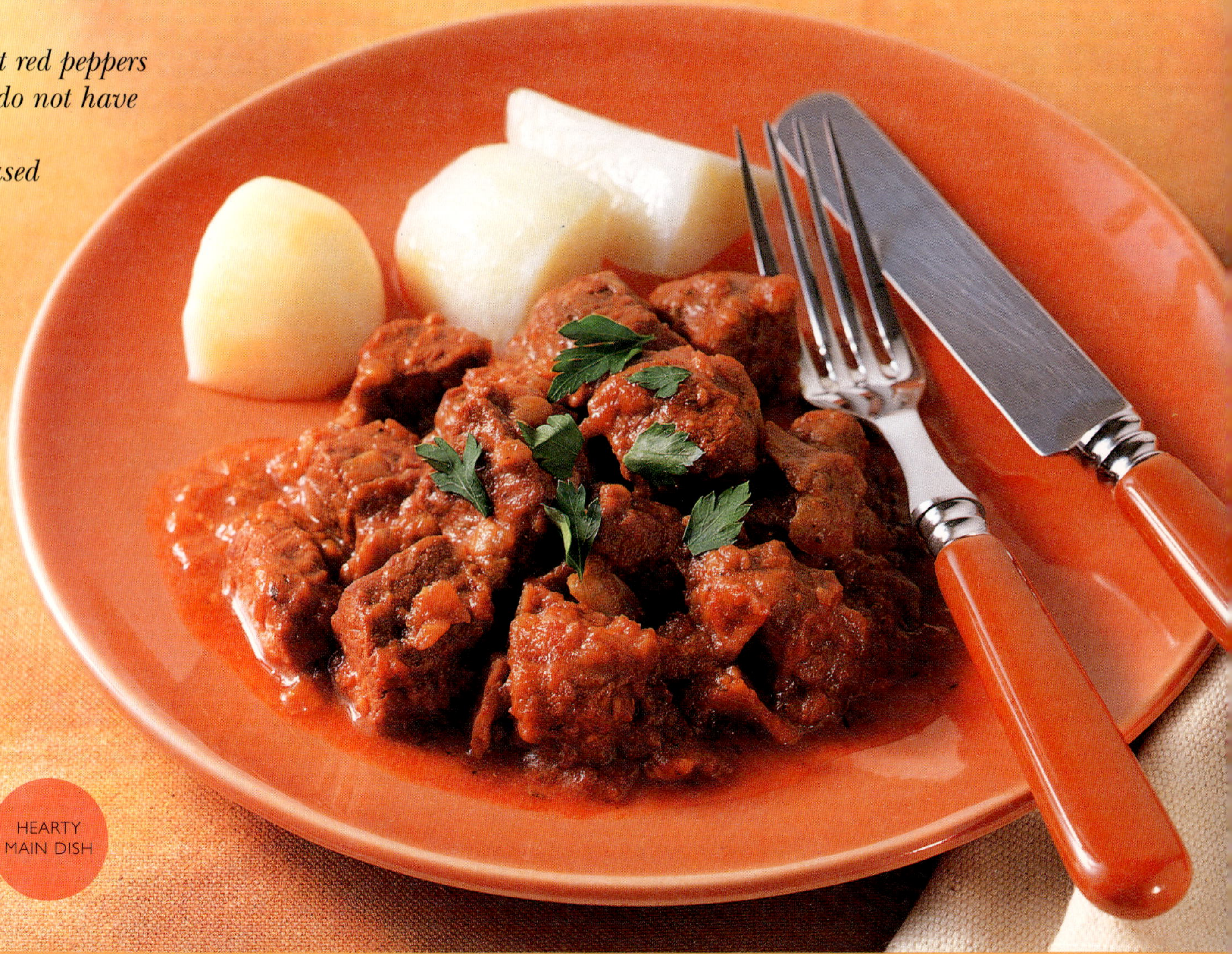

SERVING TIP

Plain boiled potatoes make a simple accompaniment to this delicious Hungarian goulash. Instant noodles, tossed in butter, and a generous dollop of soured cream, are a more elaborate alternative.

INGREDIENTS

SERVES 4

- 2 level tbsp plain flour
- 3 level tbsp paprika
- 1 level tsp salt
- ½ level tsp ground black pepper
- 900g diced stewing or braising steak
- 2 medium onions
- 8 rashers rindless, smoked back bacon
- 2 tbsp olive oil
- 2 level tsp mixed dried herbs
- 400g can chopped tomatoes
- 300ml water
- flat leaf parsley to garnish

HEARTY MAIN DISH

EQUIPMENT • LARGE FOOD BAG • SMALL SHARP KNIFE • CUTTING BOARD • KITCHEN SCISSORS • LARGE CASSEROLE WITH LID • WOODEN SPOON • CAN OPENER • MEASURING JUG

1 Put 2 tbsp flour, 3 tbsp paprika, 1 tsp salt and ½ tsp pepper into a large food bag. Add 900g diced steak, twist top of bag and shake to coat the meat.

2 With a small sharp knife, peel 2 onions (see page 10) and cut in half through the core. Dice by slicing each half along its length and then across the slices at right angles.

3 Cut 8 rashers bacon into 2.5cm pieces using kitchen scissors. Heat 2 tbsp oil in large casserole. Add onion and bacon and fry for about 5 mins, stirring occasionally.

4 Add beef, separating the pieces as you add them to the casserole. Stir fry by stirring continuously over high heat for about 2 mins until browned, to seal* the meat.

5 Add 2 tsp mixed dried herbs, contents of 400g can chopped tomatoes and 300ml water, stir well and bring to the boil. Cover and cook in a preheated oven at 170°C (325°F) mark 3 for 1½–2 hrs or until tender, stirring half way through cooking time. Serve garnished with flat leaf parsley.

*COOKING TERM
To seal meat means to cook it quickly over high heat so that it browns and the natural juices are sealed in. This makes the meat more succulent. Seal meat that is to be stewed or casseroled.

BEEF GOULASH (per serving)
• CALORIES 604 • PROTEIN 56g • CARBOHYDRATE 20g
• FAT 34g • CHOLESTEROL 172mg • SODIUM 1271mg

BAKED COD WITH MUSTARD AND CAPER SAUCE

Leaving the skin on the cod fillets makes them easier to handle and less likely to break. The crunchy cheese topping makes a delicious contrast to the delicate fish.

SERVING TIP
Serve with fresh green beans and carrots if you are feeling health conscious. For an occasional treat, serve the cod with oven-baked French fries, and relish the taste of home-made Fish and Chips.

INGREDIENTS

SERVES 4

4 cod fillets, about 125g each, with skin

salt and ground black pepper

50g plain crisps

125g grated Cheddar cheese

1 level tbsp capers

200ml crème fraîche

4 tbsp single cream

1 level tbsp wholegrain mustard

48

COOKING KNOW-HOW

How to Test to See if Fish is Done

- Fish is delicate and can easily be overcooked so always test the fish a little before the end of the recommended time. As the thickness of the fish can vary, this will reduce the chance of overcooking.
- Insert the tip of a sharp knife into the thickest part of the fish; the flesh should flake easily.
- Check the flesh is opaque in colour throughout; if the centre looks translucent, cook for a further 2 mins and test again.

"FRIED" FISH FLAVOUR

EQUIPMENT • ROASTING PAN WITH RACK • LARGE FOOD BAG • ROLLING PIN • SMALL BOWL • KITCHEN SCISSORS • MEDIUM BOWL • TABLESPOON

1 Place the 4 cod fillets, skin side down, on an oiled rack in a roasting pan. Sprinkle with salt and pepper.

2 Put 50g crisps into a large food bag, gather top to seal, extracting as much air as possible. Crush crisps lightly with a rolling pin into coarse crumbs, shaking bag occasionally.

3 Sprinkle crisps over fish, pressing in gently with your fingers.

49

4 Sprinkle 125g grated Cheddar cheese over the crumbed cod fillets, then bake in a preheated oven at 200°C (400°F) mark 6 for about 15 mins until the fish is opaque throughout.

5 Place 1 tbsp capers in the small bowl and snip into about 2mm pieces with kitchen scissors.

6 Put 200ml crème fraîche, 4 tbsp cream, 1 tbsp mustard and salt and pepper to taste in medium bowl. Add capers and stir well. Serve the sauce with the baked cod.

BAKED COD WITH MUSTARD AND CAPER SAUCE (per serving)
• CALORIES 480 • PROTEIN 33g • CARBOHYDRATE 9g
• FAT 35g • CHOLESTEROL 150mg • SODIUM 537mg

DINNER PARTY DISH

PAN-FRIED SALMON WITH TOMATO SALSA

Salmon is rightly considered the king of fish, and makes a luxurious meal for a special occasion. This recipe only takes moments to prepare and is simplicity itself – the important thing is not to overcook the fish. Prepare the tomato salsa in advance to allow the flavours to develop.

SERVING TIP
Boiled baby new potatoes (see page 69) are a classic accompaniment but brown or wild rice make good alternatives.

INGREDIENTS

SERVES 4

450g fresh plum tomatoes
8 large sprigs parsley
2 tbsp olive oil
1 tsp red wine vinegar
1 level tsp chilli sauce
salt and ground black pepper

700g salmon fillet, with skin
25g butter
1 level tsp dried tarragon
fresh tarragon to garnish

COOKING KNOW-HOW

How to Skin a Salmon Fillet

Place salmon skin side down on cutting board. Loosen skin from flesh along one short end, using a large sharp knife.

Hold knife at 45° to flesh. Using a gentle sawing motion, work knife away from you between skin and flesh. Hold skin firmly with other hand using kitchen paper to help grip.

50

1 With a small sharp knife, cut a small cross at each end of the tomatoes, place them in a medium bowl and pour boiling water over. Leave to stand for 1 min then drain through a colander.

2 Return tomatoes to bowl and cover with cold water. Peel away tomato skin using the small sharp knife. Cut in half, remove core and scoop out seeds using a teaspoon; discard seeds.

3 Using the small sharp knife, dice the tomato halves by first slicing along their length, and then across the slices at right angles. Transfer the diced tomato to the medium bowl.

4 Put 8 parsley sprigs in small bowl, snip into small pieces using kitchen scissors. Add parsley to tomatoes with 2 tbsp oil, 1 tsp vinegar, 1 tsp chilli sauce, and salt and pepper and stir well.

5 Skin 700g salmon fillet (see page 50); trim away 1cm from the thin edges of the fillet then cut crosswise into 2.5cm wide slices. Turn the pieces on their side on one layer of cling film. Cover with a second layer of cling film and pound gently using a rolling pin, until they are about 1cm thick.

6 Heat 25g butter in frying pan until foaming. Add 1 tsp tarragon and salmon; fry for about 30 secs, turn and fry for 30–60 secs longer. Serve with the juices poured over the salmon and with the tomato salsa. Garnish with fresh tarragon.

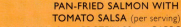

PAN-FRIED SALMON WITH TOMATO SALSA (per serving)
• CALORIES 436 • PROTEIN 33g • CARBOHYDRATE 4g
• FAT 32g • CHOLESTEROL 102mg • SODIUM 230mg

RICE

A staple food in a large part of the world, plain rice is an excellent accompaniment to a wide range of dishes. It also works well as the base for more exotic or leftover ingredients. On the stove, cooking is simple but a microwave eliminates the need for stirring.

COOKING KNOW-HOW

Plain and Flavoured Rice

Our recipe for plain white rice uses the following ingredients:

about 2.3 litres water
1 level tsp salt
350g long grain rice
15g butter

This amount will serve 4, but if you want to cook for a different number use the following guidelines:

- Allow about 50g uncooked rice per person for a side dish serving, and about 75g per person for a main dish.

- Do not cook more than 450g rice at a time, because the quantities become more difficult to handle.
- The easiest way to cook rice is in plenty of boiling salted water, similar to cooking pasta.
- Rice absorbs about 3 times its weight in water, so make sure you use a saucepan large enough to hold plenty of water.
- Although rice is usually cooked in water, stock can be used instead for added flavour when making a rice based main dish.

- Rice absorbs salt easily so do not over-salt the water.
- In general, long grain rice will take 10–12 mins to cook, brown rice (the whole grain including the bran layer) 30–35 mins.
- To test the rice is cooked, bite a grain of rice – it should be *al dente*, which means tender but retaining some bite. Alternatively, press some grains between your fingers, if they still feel hard in the centre, cook the rice a little longer and test again.

Cajun spiced rice is a main course rice dish, complete with spicy sausage and vegetables.

52

Plain white rice can be used to accompany almost any dish.

Egg fried rice is the classic partner for Chinese dishes.

1 Put about 2.3 litres water and 1 level tsp salt in large saucepan, cover and bring to the boil. Pour in 350g long grain rice.

2 Bring water back to the boil then reduce heat and simmer, uncovered, for 10–12 mins, stirring occasionally.

3 Strain the cooked rice through a sieve then stand the sieve on top of the saucepan to drain thoroughly.

4 Cut 15g butter into pieces and dot over rice. Using a fork, toss gently to separate the grains and mix in butter. If using immediately, transfer to serving dish.

VARIATIONS

CAJUN SPICED RICE

SERVES 4

Cook and drain **350g long grain rice**, and set aside in pan. Heat **1 tbsp olive oil** in frying pan. Peel and dice **1 medium onion**, add to pan and cook for 5 mins, stirring occasionally. Add **2 level tsp Jamaican Jerk seasoning**, **½ level tsp each cayenne pepper and ground ginger**, **2 level tbsp tomato ketchup**, **2 tbsp Worcestershire sauce**, and **salt and ground black pepper** to taste; cook for 2 mins. Drain one **285g jar of peppers in oil** and dice **125g chorizo sausage** into 1cm pieces and add to the cooked rice. Heat through, stirring, for about 5 mins.

EASY FRIED RICE

SERVES 4 AS AN ACCOMPANIMENT

Cook and drain **225g long grain rice** and set aside. Peel and finely chop **2.5cm piece root ginger**. Heat **1 tbsp olive oil** and **2 tbsp dark soy sauce** in frying pan. Drain one **200g can sweetcorn**. Add sweetcorn, ginger, **125g frozen peas** and stir fry over high heat for 2 mins. Add **175g cooked, peeled prawns**, the cooked rice and plenty of **salt and ground black pepper** and stir fry for 2–3 mins. Lightly beat **1 medium egg**, stir into the rice mixture and cook, stirring, for 1 min.

COOKING KNOW-HOW

Microwave Method

- Do not cook more than 350g rice at a time.
- Use double the amount of water to rice.
- Use a heatproof bowl, large enough to hold the rice as it increases in volume.
- Cover the bowl tightly with cling film and pierce it several times.
- Cook on High for about 7 mins, then on Defrost for about 8 mins for a 700 watt microwave, or check your oven handbook.
- Leave to stand for 3 mins then remove the cling film; add salt to taste and 15g butter, cut into small pieces. Toss well with a fork before serving.

53

RICE (per serving)
- CALORIES 344 • PROTEIN 6g • CARBOHYDRATE 76g
- FAT 4g • CHOLESTEROL 9mg • SODIUM 540mg

SPINACH AND PROSCIUTTO RISOTTO

When cooked, Arborio rice should be tender and have a very creamy, slightly sticky consistency. The quantity of stock given here is a guide, so have a little more at hand in case the risotto becomes too thick.

SERVING TIP
A risotto is the original one-dish meal and needs no accompaniment. Use only Arborio rice as it contains the starch needed to make the risotto creamy.

INGREDIENTS

SERVES 2–3

- 125g fresh spinach
- 1 medium onion
- 25g butter
- 1 level tsp garlic purée
- 225g Arborio rice
- 750–900ml chicken stock
- 70g prosciutto ham
- 50g grated Parmesan cheese
- salt and ground black pepper

COOKING KNOW-HOW

Stock

Stock is the basis of a good soup. It is easy to make by boiling vegetables, or meat or fish bones, in water to produce a flavoursome liquid, but it does take time.

- Stock cubes are a good standby. Use sparingly, usually one cube per 600ml of water, as they can be salty.
- Cans and jars, and fresh stocks, are available in supermarkets: they are a good substitute for home made, adding flavour and colour, but more expensive.

CLASSIC ITALIAN DISH

EQUIPMENT • COLANDER • SMALL SHARP KNIFE • CUTTING BOARD • LARGE SAUCEPAN • WOODEN SPOON • MEASURING JUG • KITCHEN SCISSORS

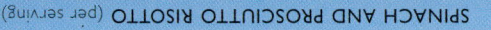

SPINACH AND PROSCIUTTO RISOTTO (per serving)
CALORIES 734 • PROTEIN 32g • CARBOHYDRATE 104g
• FAT 24g • CHOLESTEROL 65mg • SODIUM 161mg

1 Wash 125g spinach in several changes of water and drain well in colander. Remove any tough stalks.

2 Peel 1 onion (see page 10) and cut in half through core. Dice by slicing each half along its length and then across the slices at right angles.

3 Heat 25g butter in large saucepan until foaming. Add the diced onion and cook, stirring occasionally, for 5 mins.

4 Add 1 tsp garlic purée and **225g** Arborio rice, and stir for 1 min until the rice becomes translucent. Add **about 600ml** of the stock and bring to the boil.

5 Reduce heat, cover and simmer for about 5 mins stirring frequently. Stir in spinach and cook for about 5 mins, uncovered, until rice is tender and most of the stock is absorbed, adding a little more stock towards the end, if the rice becomes too thick.

6 Remove pan from heat. Cut **70g** prosciutto into small pieces. Add to pan with **50g** Parmesan and salt and pepper to taste. Return pan to heat and cook, stirring, for 1–2 mins until ham is cooked and the risotto is creamy.

PASTA CARBONARA

The classic carbonara sauce is made with cream and eggs; this quick version tastes just as delicious but is much easier and more straightforward to make.

56

SERVING TIP
Pasta makes one of the easiest complete meals; serve it on its own or with freshly baked garlic bread and a green salad.

COOKING KNOW-HOW

Pasta

- Always salt the cooking water.
- Add the pasta to boiling water, bring back to the boil and then start timing.
- Cook pasta uncovered to prevent water from boiling over.
- Test pasta a couple of minutes before the recommended time – it should be *al dente* which means tender but retaining some bite.
- Drain through a colander – shake the colander to ensure any trapped water is released.
- Toss the pasta and sauce together before serving to ensure all the pasta is coated with sauce.

INGREDIENTS

SERVES 2

1 level tsp salt	150ml milk
225g pasta shapes, such as shells or bowties	2 level tbsp grated Parmesan cheese
6 rashers rindless, smoked back bacon	ground black pepper
1 tbsp olive oil	fresh basil sprigs and grated Parmesan cheese to garnish
1 level tsp garlic purée	
200g cream cheese	

QUICK AND EASY CLASSIC

1 Half fill a large saucepan with water, add 1 tsp salt, cover and bring to the boil. Add 225g pasta, bring back to the boil then simmer, uncovered, for about 10 mins, or until *al dente* (see page 52).

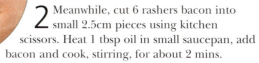

2 Meanwhile, cut 6 rashers bacon into small 2.5cm pieces using kitchen scissors. Heat 1 tbsp oil in small saucepan, add bacon and cook, stirring, for about 2 mins.

5 Return the pasta to the pan, add the sauce and stir to coat. Serve garnished with grated Parmesan cheese and basil.

3 Add 1 tsp garlic purée, 200g cream cheese, 150ml milk and 2 tbsp grated Parmesan; season with pepper. Stir over low heat until cheese has melted, then simmer for about 2 mins until thickened.

4 Drain the pasta through a colander. Shake thoroughly to make sure all the water has drained away, especially with hollow pasta shapes.

PASTA CARBONARA (per serving)
• CALORIES 1226 • PROTEIN 21g • CARBOHYDRATE 89g
• FAT 85g • CHOLESTEROL 174mg • SODIUM 1363mg

CHEESY BROCCOLI BAKE

This dish contains whisked egg whites like a soufflé but is much simpler to cook as there is no risk of the egg whites collapsing. This is an ideal winter dish which could also be made with cauliflower florets. Choose a mature Cheddar for the sauce if you like a strong cheese flavour.

COOKING KNOW-HOW

How to Separate Eggs

Have two bowls ready. Sharply tap the middle of shell on the side of one bowl. With the egg over bowl, insert your thumbs in the crack, tilt the egg and prise the shells apart. Catch yolk in the bottom shell and let the white fall into the bowl.

Carefully transfer the yolk to the empty shell half, allowing any white to fall into the bowl. Repeat to ensure that no white remains in the shell, then tip the yolk into the second bowl.

INGREDIENTS

SERVES 4

200g broccoli florets

salt

two 29g packets cheese sauce mix

300ml milk

1 level tbsp wholegrain mustard

ground black pepper

3 eggs, medium

75g grated Cheddar cheese

SERVING TIP

Grilled tomatoes are quick and easy to cook, just cut in half across the middle, and place in a foil-lined grill pan. Drizzle with a little olive oil, season with salt and pepper and grill under a hot grill until tender and slightly browned.

VEGETARIAN MAIN DISH

EQUIPMENT • MEDIUM SAUCEPAN • SMALL SHARP KNIFE • CUTTING BOARD • COLANDER • WOODEN SPOON • MEDIUM BOWL • SMALL BOWL • ELECTRIC OR ROTARY HAND WHISK • TABLESPOON • 1.7 LITRE SHALLOW, OVENPROOF DISH • BAKING SHEET

CHEESY BROCCOLI BAKE (per serving)
• CALORIES 263 • PROTEIN 17g • CARBOHYDRATE 11g
• FAT 17g • CHOLESTEROL 174mg • SODIUM 818mg

1 Half fill a medium saucepan with water and bring to the boil. With a small sharp knife, cut 200g broccoli florets into 2.5cm pieces.

2 Add the broccoli and some salt to the saucepan. Bring back to the boil and cook for 2 mins. Drain through a colander and refresh* under running cold water.

3 Put contents of two 29g packets cheese sauce, 300ml milk and 1 tbsp mustard in medium saucepan and bring to the boil, stirring. Remove from the heat, add the broccoli and salt and pepper to taste. Stir well.

4 Separate 3 eggs (see page 58), putting the whites into a medium bowl, and the yolks into a small bowl. Whisk the egg whites until they form soft peaks (see page 75).

5 Stir the egg yolks into broccoli mixture with wooden spoon. Gently fold in the egg whites with a tablespoon using a 'figure of eight' motion and being careful not to knock out any air.

6 Pour mixture into a 1.7 litre shallow, ovenproof dish. Stand dish on a baking sheet and sprinkle 75g Cheddar cheese on top. Bake in a preheated oven at 180°C (350°F) mark 4 for about 45 mins. Check after 30 mins – if top is golden, cover loosely with foil for the remaining cooking time. Serve immediately.

*COOKING TERM
To refresh vegetables, drain the vegetables through a colander, and hold under running cold water. This cools them quickly, stopping the cooking process, and helps retain their colour.

ROASTED VEGETABLES

A mixture of roasted vegetables is a versatile dish. On its own, it can be eaten hot or cold or prepared as a bake. It also can be used as a topping for baked potatoes and pizza, or be added to a ready-made pasta sauce and served with your favourite pasta.

Roasted vegetables Serve this delicious mélange of vegetables hot or refrigerate and serve as part of a summer buffet.

VARIATIONS

VEGETABLE PASTA BAKE
SERVES 4

Cook **175g pasta shapes** in boiling salted water and drain well. In a large saucepan, gently heat together **150g cream cheese with garlic and herbs** and **150ml milk**. Remove from heat, stir in pasta and **roasted vegetables**. Pour into a 1.7 litre shallow ovenproof dish. Mix **125g grated Cheddar cheese** and **25g grated Parmesan cheese** and sprinkle over the top. Stand dish on baking sheet and bake in a preheated oven at 200°C (400°F) mark 6 for 20–30 mins or until golden.

VEGETABLE PIZZA
SERVES 2

Spread **half the roasted vegetables** over a 23–25.5cm pizza base (see page 24). Drain and thinly slice **125g mozzarella cheese** and place evenly over the pizza. Bake in a preheated oven at 200°C (400°F) mark 6 for 15–20 mins.

INGREDIENTS
SERVES 4

1 red pepper

1 yellow pepper

1 medium aubergine

2 medium onions

3 courgettes

2 level tsp dried mixed herbs

salt and ground black pepper

5 tbsp olive oil

SERVE HOT OR COLD

EQUIPMENT • SMALL SHARP KNIFE • CUTTING BOARD • ROASTING PAN • LARGE SHARP KNIFE • TABLESPOON

1 Cut 1 red and 1 yellow pepper in half along their length using a small sharp knife. Remove core, seeds and any white membrane. Cut into 2.5cm cubes. Place in a roasting pan.

2 Trim stalk from 1 aubergine. Cut in half along length then cut each half along length into four pieces with large sharp knife. Cut into 1cm pieces. Add to the roasting pan.

3 Peel 2 onions (see page 10) and cut in half through the core with small sharp knife. Thinly slice each half along its length and add to roasting pan.

COOKING KNOW-HOW

Peppers and Aubergines

- Peppers are available green, red, yellow and orange in colour. They have a sweet flavour and are eaten raw or cooked; discard the seeds and white membrane before using.
- Although some aubergines are white, the most common is the purple variety. Unlike peppers, they are always eaten cooked, and the seeds of the vegetable are edible.
- Choose peppers and aubergines with smooth shiny skins that have no signs of bruising. They should feel firm and heavy for their size.

4 Trim the ends of 3 courgettes. Cut in half along their length then cut into 1cm thick slices. Add to the vegetables in the roasting pan.

5 Sprinkle 2 tsp dried herbs over the vegetables, season well with salt and pepper to taste and drizzle with 5 tbsp olive oil. Stir well then roast in a preheated oven at 200°C (400°F) mark 6 for 40–50 mins or until tender and slightly charred, stirring twice during cooking.

ROASTED VEGETABLES (per serving)
- CALORIES 194 • PROTEIN 4g • CARBOHYDRATE 13g
- FAT 15g • CHOLESTEROL 0mg • SODIUM 7mg

POTATO AND CELERIAC GRATIN

These two root vegetables, potato and celeriac, complement each other well. Particularly delicious as an accompaniment to the Roast Leg of Lamb, see page 40, this gratin can also make a filling vegetarian meal for two.

INGREDIENTS

SERVES 4

450g large potatoes

225g celeriac

1 medium onion

salt and ground black pepper

284ml carton double cream

150ml milk

1 level tsp garlic purée

COOKING KNOW-HOW

Celeriac

This knobbly root vegetable has a strong celery flavour and tough outer skin that should always be removed before using. Store in the refrigerator for up to 3 weeks. Any leftovers can be used in soups, boiled and mashed with other root vegetables such as potatoes, carrots, swede and parsnips, or grated and added to salads.

SERVING TIP
Cooked in an attractive baking dish, it can be served straight from the oven.

VEGETABLE
SIDE DISH

EQUIPMENT • SMALL SHARP KNIFE • CUTTING BOARD • LARGE BOWL • COLANDER • 1.7 LITRE SHALLOW OVENPROOF DISH • SMALL SAUCEPAN
• WOODEN SPOON • FOIL • BAKING SHEET

1 Scrub 450g large potatoes but do not peel. Slice thinly and transfer to large bowl of cold water.

2 Cut 225g celeriac into large pieces. Cut away the skin and thinly slice the flesh. Add to the potato slices in the bowl.

3 Peel 1 medium onion (see page 10) and cut in half through the core. Cut each half into thin slices along its length.

4 Drain potatoes and celeriac through a colander then return them to the bowl. Add onion and plenty of salt and pepper and toss well.

5 Reserve about 12 large slices of potato for the top. Tip remaining vegetables into a 1.7 litre shallow, ovenproof dish. Spread them out into even layers to fill the dish, then cover with the reserved potato slices.

6 Put the contents of 284ml carton cream, 150ml milk and 1 tsp garlic purée in a small saucepan. Bring to the boil, stirring. Pour over the vegetables. Cover tightly with foil. Place dish on baking sheet and bake in a preheated oven at 150°C (300°F) mark 2 for 1 hour. Remove foil and cook for a further 1–1¼ hours or until vegetables are tender and golden.

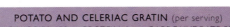

POTATO AND CELERIAC GRATIN (per serving)
• CALORIES 450 • PROTEIN 6g • CARBOHYDRATE 27g
• FAT 36g • CHOLESTEROL 98mg • SODIUM 107mg

Baked Potatoes

A baked potato, cut open and served with butter, is a simple-to-prepare snack or accompaniment. Adding one of our toppings, however, can transform it into a main meal. When making more than one, choose potatoes that are evenly sized so that they take the same time to cook. Avoid ones with any blemishes or bruising.

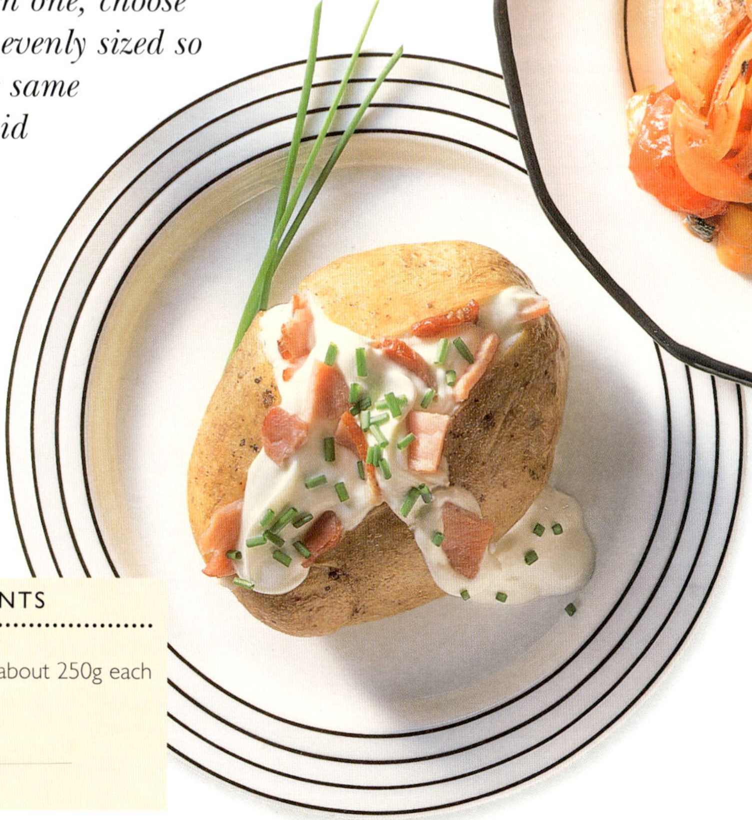

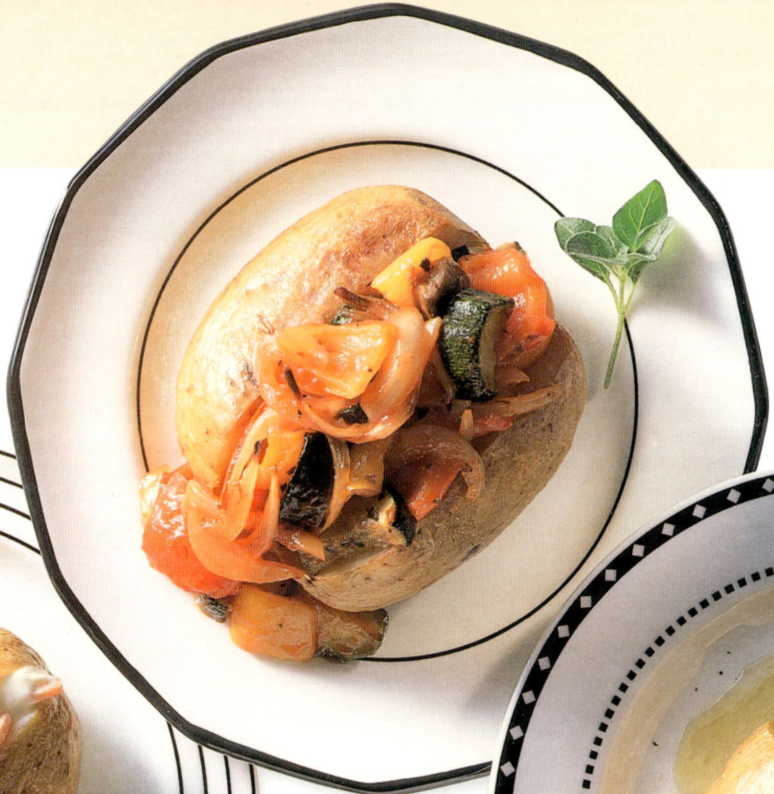

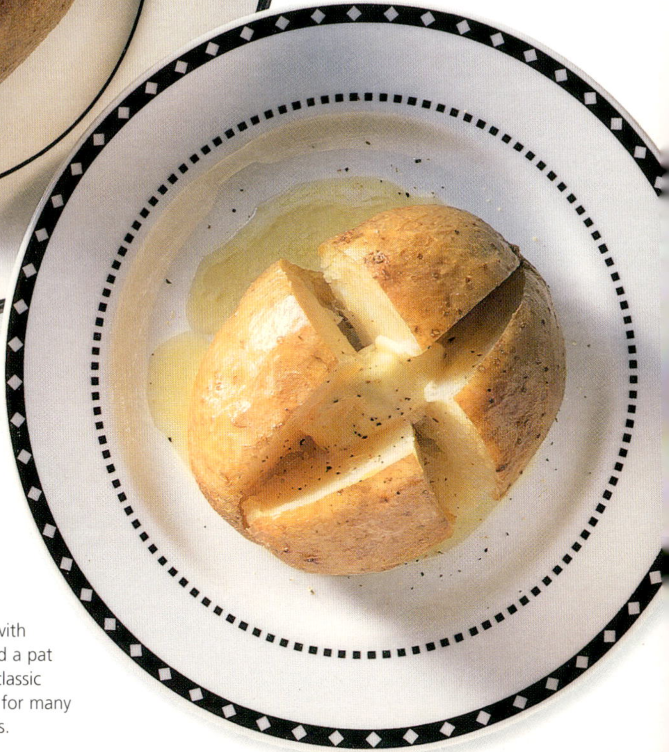

Soured cream and bacon baked potato makes an accompaniment or snack. The crunchy bacon and the smooth soured cream make a tasty contrast.

Chilli vegetable baked potato makes a filling vegetarian meal.

Baked Potato with black pepper and a pat of butter is the classic accompaniment for many meats and salads.

INGREDIENTS

SERVES 2

- 2 large baking potatoes, about 250g each
- 1 tsp olive oil
- about 50g butter
- ground black pepper

EQUIPMENT • FORK • PASTRY BRUSH • SMALL BOWL • SMALL SHARP KNIFE

1 Scrub 2 large potatoes about 250g each, and pat dry. Prick the potatoes all over with a fork.

2 To crisp the skins, brush with the olive oil. Place directly on shelf in centre of a preheated oven at 200°C (400°F) mark 6 for 1–1¼ hours, or until tender.

4 Cut the potato in half, or cut a cross in the top, and prise the potato open slightly so that the inside is exposed. Serve with butter and ground black pepper. Alternatively, top with a filling of your choice.

3 Insert the tip of a small sharp knife into the centre of the potato, there should be no resistance. The potato should also 'give' slightly when gently squeezed.

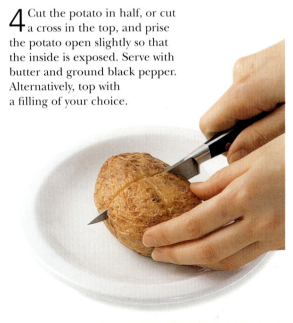

VARIATIONS

CHILLI VEGETABLE BAKED POTATOES
SERVES 2

If you have roasted vegetables (see page 60) left over, you can make the following topping. Prepare and cook **2 baked potatoes**. In a medium saucepan, gently heat together about **350g roasted vegetables**, **4 level tbsp tomato ketchup** and **2 level tsp chilli sauce**. Make one cut in the top of each baked potato, top with **a little butter** and the vegetable mixture.

SOURED CREAM AND BACON BAKED POTATOES
SERVES 2

Prepare and cook **2 baked potatoes**. Using kitchen scissors, snip about **4 chives** onto kitchen paper. Set aside. Grill **2 rashers rindless smoked back bacon** on rack of grill pan. Snip bacon into small pieces with kitchen scissors. Cut a cross in the top of each baked potato. Spoon over contents of **142ml carton soured cream** and top with bacon bits. Garnish with snipped chives.

COOKING KNOW-HOW

How to Bake Potatoes

- A potato baker is a spike which conducts the heat of the oven through to the centre of the potatoes, helping them to cook more evenly. The central handle makes it easier to transfer them from the oven.
- If you prefer your baked potatoes with soft skin, rather than crispy, wrap each potato in foil instead of brushing it with oil in Step 2.

- Microwaving potatoes also produces a softer baked potato, but saves time. To microwave, prick the skin, wrap each potato in a piece of kitchen paper. Stand the potatoes, evenly spaced, around the edge of the microwave turntable and cook on High for 8–10 mins for a 700 watt microwave, or check your microwave handbook.

BAKED POTATOES (per serving)
• CALORIES 385 • PROTEIN 5g • CARBOHYDRATE 43g
• FAT 22g • CHOLESTEROL 58mg • SODIUM 205mg

COLD
MAIN DISH

CURRIED CHICKEN SALAD

For an updated variation of Coronation chicken, the combination of soured cream, apricots and curry paste creates a delicate, mildly spiced and creamy dish. For a lower-fat alternative, choose light mayonnaise.

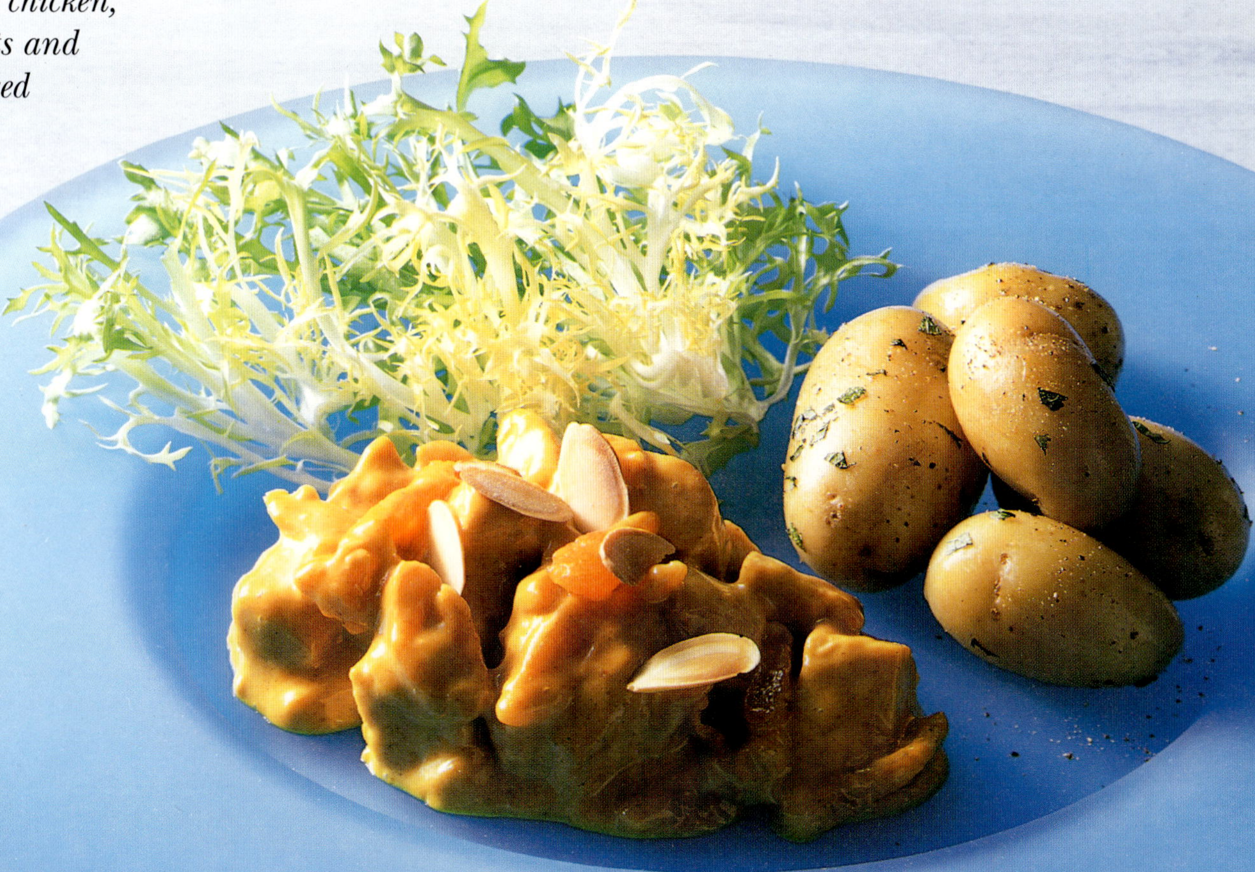

INGREDIENTS

SERVES 4

200g jar mayonnaise

4 level tbsp soured cream

2 level tbsp **each** mild curry paste and apricot jam

salt and ground black pepper

75g no-soak dried apricots

25g flaked almonds

450g boneless, cooked chicken breasts or thighs

SERVING TIP
▶ Warm minted new potatoes and lettuce leaves are good choices for a summer menu.

99

1 Put 200g mayonnaise and 4 tbsp soured cream into a large bowl. Stir in 2 tbsp curry paste, 2 tbsp apricot jam and a generous amount of salt and pepper.

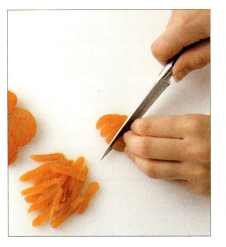

2 With a small sharp knife, cut 75g apricots along their length into fine strips. Add to mayonnaise mixture.

3 Line a grill pan with foil. Scatter 25g flaked almonds over the foil. Toast under hot grill until golden, shaking the pan to toast both sides.

6 Add the chicken pieces to the curry mayonnaise. Stir well to coat. Serve garnished with the reserved toasted almonds sprinkled on top.

4 Let the toasted almonds cool slightly then reserve a few almonds for garnish; add the remainder to the mayonnaise mixture.

5 With your fingers, skin 450g chicken breasts or thighs and, with the small sharp knife, cut the meat into bite-size pieces.

CURRIED CHICKEN SALAD (per serving)
• CALORIES 614 • PROTEIN 31g • CARBOHYDRATE 12g
• FAT 49g • CHOLESTEROL 106mg • SODIUM 368mg

Niçoise Salad

This Mediterranean inspired main dish pairs canned tuna and fresh vegetables. Canned tuna is available in oil or brine. The flavour is similar but the texture of the oil version is slightly better. If you are cutting down on fat, however, choose the low-fat option of tuna in brine.

68

INGREDIENTS

SERVES 4

700g small new potatoes, washed

salt

2 eggs

3 sticks celery

two 200g cans tuna in oil or brine

125g cherry tomatoes

Classic French Dressing (see page 71)

about 8 pitted black olives

celery leaves to garnish

SERVING TIP

This salad can be served straight away while the potatoes and eggs are still warm. To serve cold, cover and chill for about 1 hour.

COOKING KNOW-HOW

How to Boil Eggs and Vegetables

- Fill saucepan half full with water.
- Bring water to a rolling boil – large bubbles – with the lid on, before adding vegetables; add eggs to cold water then bring to the boil.
- Add a little salt with vegetables, and any extra seasoning after they are cooked.
- When the water has returned to the boil, begin timing and reduce the heat so the water just simmers – when the large bubbles are replaced by small bubbles coming up to the surface.
- Always simmer **uncovered** to prevent the water boiling over.

SUMMER FAVOURITE

EQUIPMENT • MEDIUM SAUCEPAN • LARGE SPOON • COLANDER • SMALL BOWL • CUTTING BOARD • SMALL SHARP KNIFE • CAN OPENER • SIEVE • FORKS

1 Half fill a medium saucepan with water, cover and bring to the boil. Add 700g new potatoes and 1 tsp salt. Return to boil and simmer for 10 mins or until tender. Drain in a colander. Add to serving dish.

2 Place 2 eggs in pan, cover with cold water. Bring to the boil, reduce heat, simmer for 10 mins, then drain in colander. Cool in cold water. Gently crack shells on counter; peel eggs, and transfer to cold water.

3 Rinse 3 sticks celery to remove any dirt. Lay them flat on a cutting board, hollow side up. Trim 1cm from the ends of each celery stick, then cut them crosswise into slices about 3mm thick. Add the sliced celery to the serving dish.

4 Turn out two 200g cans of tuna into a sieve placed over a small bowl. Leave for about 1–2 mins to drain then, using two forks, carefully separate flakes. Add tuna to the serving dish, using forks to toss ingredients lightly.

5 Halve 125g cherry tomatoes by cutting down through core ends. Scatter them over rest of ingredients in serving dish. Drizzle Classic French dressing over tuna mixture to coat evenly.

6 Cut each egg in half along its length then cut each in half again. Place the egg quarters on top of the tuna salad, and sprinkle about 8 olives over. Serve straight away or chill first, if you like. Garnish with celery leaves.

NIÇOISE SALAD (per serving)
• CALORIES 508 • PROTEIN 25g • CARBOHYDRATE 30g
• FAT 33g • CHOLESTEROL 129mg • SODIUM 615mg

ORIENTAL NOODLE SALAD

A salad can be as simple as a collection of green leaves mixed with one of the dressings below, or a far more exotic combination of vegetables, beans or noodles – as the warm salad shown here.

SERVING TIP
Garnish with sliced spring onions, see page 45, and sprinkle with chopped peanuts, chopped as for the ginger in Step 1.

SALAD VARIATIONS

LEMON VEGETABLE SALAD
SERVES 4

Half fill a large saucepan with water, add **½ level tsp salt** and bring to the boil. Add **500g small washed new potatoes**. Bring back to the boil and simmer for about 5 mins. Add **125g each of peas, trimmed French beans, baby carrots and baby sweetcorn**. Bring back to the boil and simmer for about 5 mins or until just tender; drain and transfer to a large bowl. Pour the **Creamy Lemon Dressing** (see page 71) over the salad and toss well. Leave to marinate uncovered for 30 mins, stirring occasionally. Serve in a salad bowl, if you like.

MIXED BEAN SALAD
SERVES 4

Drain **two 420g cans mixed beans** through a sieve and transfer to a large bowl. Cut **125g cherry tomatoes** in half, dice **125g feta cheese** into 1 cm cubes and add to bowl. Pour the **Italian Dressing** (see page 71) over the salad and toss well. Serve in a salad bowl, if you like, garnished with **basil leaves**.

INGREDIENTS

SERVES 4

For the dressing:
2.5cm piece of fresh root ginger
120ml olive oil
1 tbsp white wine vinegar
2 tbsp dark soy sauce
1 tbsp sherry
ground black pepper

For the salad:
½ level tsp salt
250g packet egg noodles
3 finely sliced spring onions, to garnish
25g roughly chopped salted peanuts, to garnish

COOKING KNOW-HOW

Quick Method of Mixing Dressing

Put all the ingredients in a screw top jar (make sure the inside of the lid is plastic coated) and shake well. The dressing will keep in the refrigerator up to 5 days.

EQUIPMENT • SMALL SHARP KNIFE • CUTTING BOARD • LARGE SHARP KNIFE • SMALL BOWL • FORKS • LARGE SAUCEPAN • COLANDER

TASTE OF THE EAST

1 With a small sharp knife, peel a 2.5cm piece of fresh root ginger and cut into small pieces. Finely chop ginger: hold the tip of a large sharp knife firmly to the cutting board and raise and lower the handle working the blade over ginger pieces.

2 Whisk 120ml olive oil and 1 tbsp white wine vinegar. Add chopped ginger, 2 tbsp dark soy sauce, 1 tbsp sherry and pepper to taste. Whisk and set aside.

3 Half fill a large saucepan with water, add ½ tsp salt and bring to the boil. Add a 250g packet egg noodles, and cook following pack instructions.

4 Drain the cooked egg noodles through a colander and return to the empty pan.

5 Pour in the Oriental dressing and toss well. Serve immediately garnished with 3 sliced spring onions and 25g chopped peanuts.

DRESSING VARIATIONS

CLASSIC FRENCH DRESSING

Place **120ml olive oil**, **1 tbsp white wine vinegar**, **1 level tbsp wholegrain mustard** and **salt and ground black pepper** to taste in a small bowl and whisk with a fork or small balloon whisk. Pour the dressing over mixed salad leaves and toss lightly.

ITALIAN DRESSING

Whisk together **120ml olive oil** and **1 tbsp white wine vinegar**. Add **1 tbsp red pesto** and **salt and ground black pepper** to taste and whisk in a small bowl using a fork or small balloon whisk until all the ingredients are blended.

CREAMY LEMON DRESSING

Finely grate the rind of **1 lemon**; cut the lemon in half and squeeze **2 tbsp lemon juice** into a small bowl. Add **120ml olive oil**, **1 level tbsp wholegrain mustard**, **2 tbsp single or double cream** and the lemon rind. Add **salt and ground black pepper** to taste and whisk well with a fork or small balloon whisk.

COOKING KNOW-HOW

Green Salad Leaves

Bags of pre-washed mixed leaves are widely available; these are not only convenient but also a good way of trying different leaves, such as radicchio, frisée, oak leaf and lollo rosso, that may be less familiar. To add some quick extras to them, toss in cherry tomatoes, bought croûtons, sliced radishes or olives with the dressing of your choice.

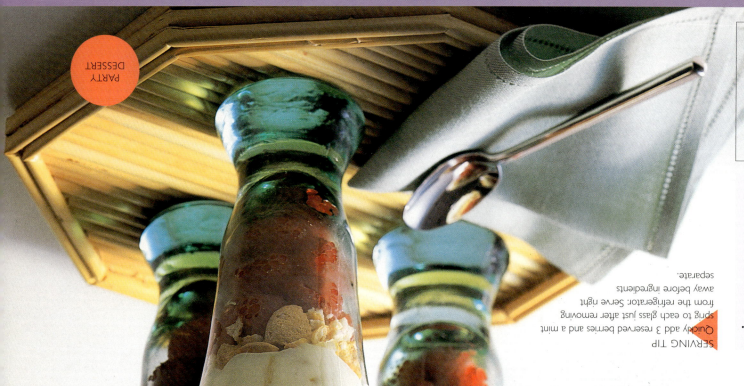

PARTY DESSERT

RASPBERRY RATAFIA CRUNCH

This quick-and-easy dessert lends itself to a variety of fresh and frozen fruit. Use fresh raspberries when they are in season and most plentiful and frozen ones in the winter. Other fruits like halved seedless black grapes, or stoned and diced plums and peaches will work well also.

INGREDIENTS

SERVES 4

75g ratafia biscuits
1 piece of stem ginger in syrup, about 25g
250g tub mascarpone cheese
4 level tbsp soured cream
142ml carton single cream
350g fresh raspberries
mint leaves to decorate

SERVING TIP
Quickly add 3 reserved berries and a mint sprig to each glass just after removing from the refrigerator. Serve right away before ingredients separate.

INGREDIENT NOTE

Stem ginger in syrup is sold in jars and normally found in the baking section of the supermarket. Leftover chopped stem ginger can be stirred into yoghurt or spooned over your favourite breakfast cereal, while the syrup can be poured over ice cream, pancakes or fresh fruit.

72

1 Put 75g biscuits in a large food bag. Gather up and hold the top of the bag, making sure all the air is extracted, then lay it flat on the counter. Lightly crush the biscuits by hitting them with a rolling pin.

2 On cutting board, slice 25g piece stem ginger in half with a small sharp knife. Place one half cut-side down and thinly slice. Gather pieces together and cut across into very small even pieces. Repeat for the other half.

3 Place 250g mascarpone in a medium bowl. Using a wooden spoon, beat in 4 tbsp soured cream. Very gradually add contents of 142ml carton cream, beating well after each addition. Stir in the chopped ginger.

4 Put 12 of the best looking raspberries on a plate, loosely cover and refrigerate until required for decorating. Place a **quarter** of the remaining raspberries into the bottom of each glass.

6 Sprinkle the remaining biscuits on top. Cover tightly with cling film and chill for about 2 hours before serving.

5 Divide the crushed biscuits into two equal piles. Sprinkle **half** the biscuits over the berries in each glass. Divide the mascarpone mixture between the glasses. Smooth the surface, right to the edges of the glass, using the back of a teaspoon, to cover berry and biscuit layer completely.

RASPBERRY RATAFIA CRUNCH (per serving)
• CALORIES 496 • PROTEIN 5g • CARBOHYDRATE 29g
• FAT 40g • CHOLESTEROL 94mg • SODIUM 167mg

MOCHA MOUSSE

This creamy dessert will satisfy the most ardent chocoholic. It can be made up to two days beforehand: when it is set, just cover it tightly with cling film and refrigerate. Decorate it just before serving.

INGREDIENTS

SERVES 4

200g bar plain chocolate

1 tbsp boiling water

5 eggs, medium

1 level tbsp instant coffee granules

142ml carton double cream to decorate

a little cocoa to decorate

SERVING TIP
A dollop of whipped cream and a sprinkling of cocoa is the perfect topping. Whipped cream in aerosol cans is widely available to make piped rosettes.

PREPARE AHEAD

COOKING KNOW-HOW

How to Melt Chocolate

- Melt chocolate very slowly in a bowl over simmering water. If it gets too hot, it can burn.
- Don't let any water splash into the bowl as this can cause the chocolate to become stiff.
- Make sure that the bottom of the bowl does not touch the water.
- Only stir the chocolate once it has softened.

To microwave:
- Use a microwavable bowl.
- Melt chocolate uncovered.
- Always use a low power setting.
- Chocolate will retain its shape when hot, so check the mixture with a spoon every 30 secs to see if it is soft.

1 Half fill a large saucepan with water and bring to the boil. Reduce heat and simmer. Break 200g bar chocolate into a large bowl and place over pan of water until melted, about 10 mins.

2 Remove bowl from heat and allow to cool slightly. Separate 5 eggs (see page 58), catching the whites in a medium bowl and placing 4 of the yolks in a small bowl. Discard the extra yolk. Beat the 4 egg yolks into the chocolate mixture.

3 In a small bowl blend together 1 tbsp instant coffee granules and 1 tbsp boiling water. Add to the chocolate mixture. Whisk the egg whites until they form soft peaks.*

4 Stir about 2 tbsp of egg white into the chocolate mixture to lighten it. Fold in the remaining egg whites using a figure of eight motion, being careful not to knock out any air.

*COOKING TERM
When egg whites are whisked to the soft peak stage, they should just be stiff enough to hold their own shape. When the whisk is lifted from the bowl the peaks should just flop over at the top. For stiff peaks, the egg white peaks will stand upright and not fall over.

5 Spoon the mousse into four 200ml cups or dishes. Chill, uncovered, for about 2 hours until set. Whip contents of 142ml carton double cream until stiff; spoon on top of each mousse. Sprinkle a little cocoa over to decorate.

TECHNIQUE TIP
If you are feeling really adventurous, use a piping bag or syringe, fitted with a star nozzle, to create elegantly piped rosettes of whipped cream. Easy!

MOCHA MOUSSE (per serving)
• CALORIES 519 • PROTEIN 11g • CARBOHYDRATE 34g
• FAT 39g • CHOLESTEROL 291mg • SODIUM 114mg

FRUDITÉ WITH CHOCOLATE SAUCE AND ORANGE CREAM

A fruity version of the more well-known vegetable crudité, this makes a delicious snack or finish to a special meal.

SERVING TIP

Let each person serve themselves by spooning a selection of fruit onto their plate, and topping it with orange cream and a drizzle of warm chocolate sauce. Delicious!

COOKING KNOW-HOW

How to Remove Rind from a Grater

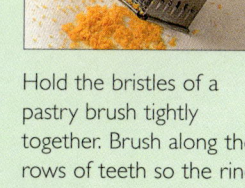

After grating citrus fruit, rind will remain in the grater: hold it over a piece of kitchen paper and scrape away the rind inside the grater with a round-bladed knife.

Hold the bristles of a pastry brush tightly together. Brush along the rows of teeth so the rind falls onto the kitchen paper. Remove rind inside the grater again.

INGREDIENTS

SERVES 4

1 large orange

142ml carton extra thick double cream

2 ripe pears

2 medium bananas

175g strawberries

150g plain chocolate

25g butter

5 tbsp double cream

SUMMER DESSERT

EQUIPMENT • GRATER • KITCHEN PAPER • ROUND-BLADED KNIFE • TEASPOON • MEDIUM BOWL • SMALL SHARP KNIFE • CUTTING BOARD • SMALL SAUCEPAN • WOODEN SPOON

1 Grate rind from 1 large orange being careful not to include any white pith (see page 76). Stir into contents of 142ml carton extra thick double cream. Put in serving dish, cover and chill until required.

2 Cut a small slice off each end of the orange. Stand orange upright onto cut base to steady it. Starting at the top, cut away a slice of peel and white pith, working down the orange to the base, using a sawing action. Turn the orange slightly and continue removing the peel all the way around.

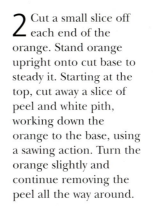

3 Turn orange on its side and cut crosswise into thin slices. Discard any pips. Transfer the orange slices to the serving platter.

4 Wash 2 ripe pears but do not peel. Cut them into quarters along their length. Remove the cores and cut the flesh lengthwise into thick slices. Add to the serving platter.

5 Peel 2 bananas. Trim ends and cut diagonally into 1cm slices; wash 175g strawberries and pat dry with kitchen paper. Add to serving platter.

6 Break 150g chocolate into a small saucepan. Add 25g butter and 5 tbsp double cream. Heat very gently, undisturbed, until chocolate softens, then stir until completely melted. Remove from heat and beat with a wooden spoon until smooth. Serve warm with the fruit platter and orange cream.

**FRUDITE WITH CHOCOLATE SAUCE
AND ORANGE CREAM** (per serving)
• CALORIES 619 • PROTEIN 4g • CARBOHYDRATE 51g
• FAT 45g • CHOLESTEROL 96mg • SODIUM 81mg

PLUM NUT TART

Freshly stoned plums and nuts tucked up in a pastry surround is delicious fresh out of the oven or served cool. Ready made pastry is an excellent alternative to making your own; look for it in the chill cabinet or freezer section of your supermarket.

SERVING TIP
Glazing the pastry with milk and sugar gives the tart an appetizing sheen. For a special treat, accompany it with fresh or whipped cream, or with a scoop of ice cream.

COOKING KNOW-HOW

How to Stone a Plum

Cut around the plum, down to the stone, following the natural crease. Twist the two sections in opposite directions to separate.

Cut around the stone with the tip of a small sharp knife. Remove and discard the stones.

INGREDIENTS

SERVES 4

300g ripe plums

2 tbsp dark rum

25g hazelnuts

about 1 level tbsp plain flour

250g ready made short crust pastry, at room temperature

2 level tbsp caster sugar

1 tbsp milk

SERVE WARM OR COLD

1 Stone 300g ripe plums (see page 78) and cut each half lengthwise into thick slices. Put slices in medium bowl and stir in 2 tbsp dark rum.

2 Line grill pan with foil. Scatter 25g hazelnuts over foil. Toast under a hot grill until golden then transfer to cutting board and roughly chop. Hold tip of large sharp knife firmly to the board, raise and lower handle working the blade over the nuts.

3 Sprinkle about 1 tbsp flour on the counter to stop the underside of the pastry sticking and flour the rolling pin to stop it sticking to the pastry. Make a ball of 250g ready made short crust pastry then roll into a 30.5cm round by turning the pastry a quarter turn after each roll. This will help to keep the pastry's shape.

4 Lightly grease a baking sheet with butter or oil. Lift the pastry onto the baking sheet; spoon the plums into the centre, leaving a 5cm border around the edge. Sprinkle **1 tbsp** caster sugar and all the chopped nuts over the plums.

5 Bring the pastry edges up and over the fruit, pleating it where necessary, leaving a gap in the centre showing the filling.

6 Brush the pastry edge with 1 tbsp milk, sprinkle the remaining 1 tbsp sugar over the top of the tart, then bake in a preheated oven at 180°C (350°F) mark 4 for 30–40 mins or until golden.

PLUM NUT TART (per serving)
• CALORIES 383 • PROTEIN 5g • CARBOHYDRATE 40g
• FAT 2g • CHOLESTEROL 1mg • SODIUM 104mg

CRUMBLES

A crunchy topping over a fruity base lends itself to many combinations. Apple and Maple is an old favourite given a new twist, while Spiced Banana and Tropical Fruit are two very contemporary variations.

VARIATIONS

TROPICAL FRUIT CRUMBLE WITH COCONUT
SERVES 4–6

Make **crumble topping** as in Steps 1 to 3. Line a grill pan with foil; scatter **25g desiccated coconut** over foil and toast under a hot grill until golden. Cool slightly then stir into crumble mixture. Drain **425g can of tropical fruit salad** and **425g can of mango slices** and place in a 1.1 litre shallow ovenproof dish. Cut **2 passion fruit** in half, scoop out the seeds into the dish, using a teaspoon. Spoon the crumble over to cover the fruit. Stand the dish on a baking sheet and bake in a preheated oven at 200°C (400°F) mark 6 for 30–40 mins.

SPICED BANANA CRUMBLE
SERVES 4

Make **crumble topping** as in Steps 1 to 3. Peel **2 large bananas** and cut into thick slices; place in a 1.1 litre shallow ovenproof dish. Snip **50g no-soak dried apricots** into small pieces; sprinkle over banana. Spoon contents of **411g jar mincemeat** over fruit. Stir **1 level tsp mixed spice** into crumble, then spoon over mincemeat to cover completely. Stand dish on a baking sheet and bake in a preheated oven at 200°C (400°F) mark 6 for 30–40 mins.

Spiced banana crumble (top right) is delicious with ice cream.

Apple and maple crumble (right) and illustrated on page 81, is served with an English classic – custard.

Tropical fruit crumble with coconut is complemented by whipped cream.

INGREDIENTS
SERVES 4–6

For the crumble topping:
175g plain flour
75g butter, at room temperature
50g demerara sugar

For the apple and maple filling:
4 tbsp maple syrup
2 level tbsp lemon curd
75g sultanas
875g Bramley apples

80

3 Stir 50g demerara sugar into the flour mixture using a round-bladed knife.

1 To make the crumble, put 175g plain flour into a large bowl. Cut 75g butter into 4–6 pieces and add to bowl.

2 Rub the butter into the flour by rubbing thumbs over fingertips, lifting the flour as you work. Continue until the mixture resembles fine breadcrumbs. Check the butter is completely rubbed in by shaking the bowl, any large lumps will rise to the surface.

4 For apple and maple filling, put 4 tbsp maple syrup, 2 tbsp lemon curd and 75g sultanas in a medium bowl. Cut 875g Bramley apples into quarters. Stand each piece of apple on one end and cut away the core.

5 Stand each piece of apple on one end and cut away the peel working from the top, being careful not to include any flesh. Cut the apple flesh into 1–2cm pieces and add to the maple syrup mixture. Toss well to coat the apple evenly then spoon into a 1.1 litre shallow ovenproof dish.

6 Press the apple down and spoon the crumble topping over to cover the fruit. Stand the dish on a baking sheet and bake in a preheated oven at 200°C (400°F) mark 6 for 30–40 mins.

APPLE AND MAPLE CRUMBLE (per serving)
• CALORIES 526 • PROTEIN 5g • CARBOHYDRATE 95g
• FAT 17g • CHOLESTEROL 43mg • SODIUM 207mg

BUTTERED BRIOCHE PUDDING

Traditionally made with day-old bread, our up-to-the-minute version relies on a crispy bun to soak up the custard. You can make the pudding the day before if you like but bake it about 30 minutes before eating.

SERVING TIP
Delicious on its own, this pudding makes a richer dessert if you add spoonfuls of fromage fraîs or single cream.

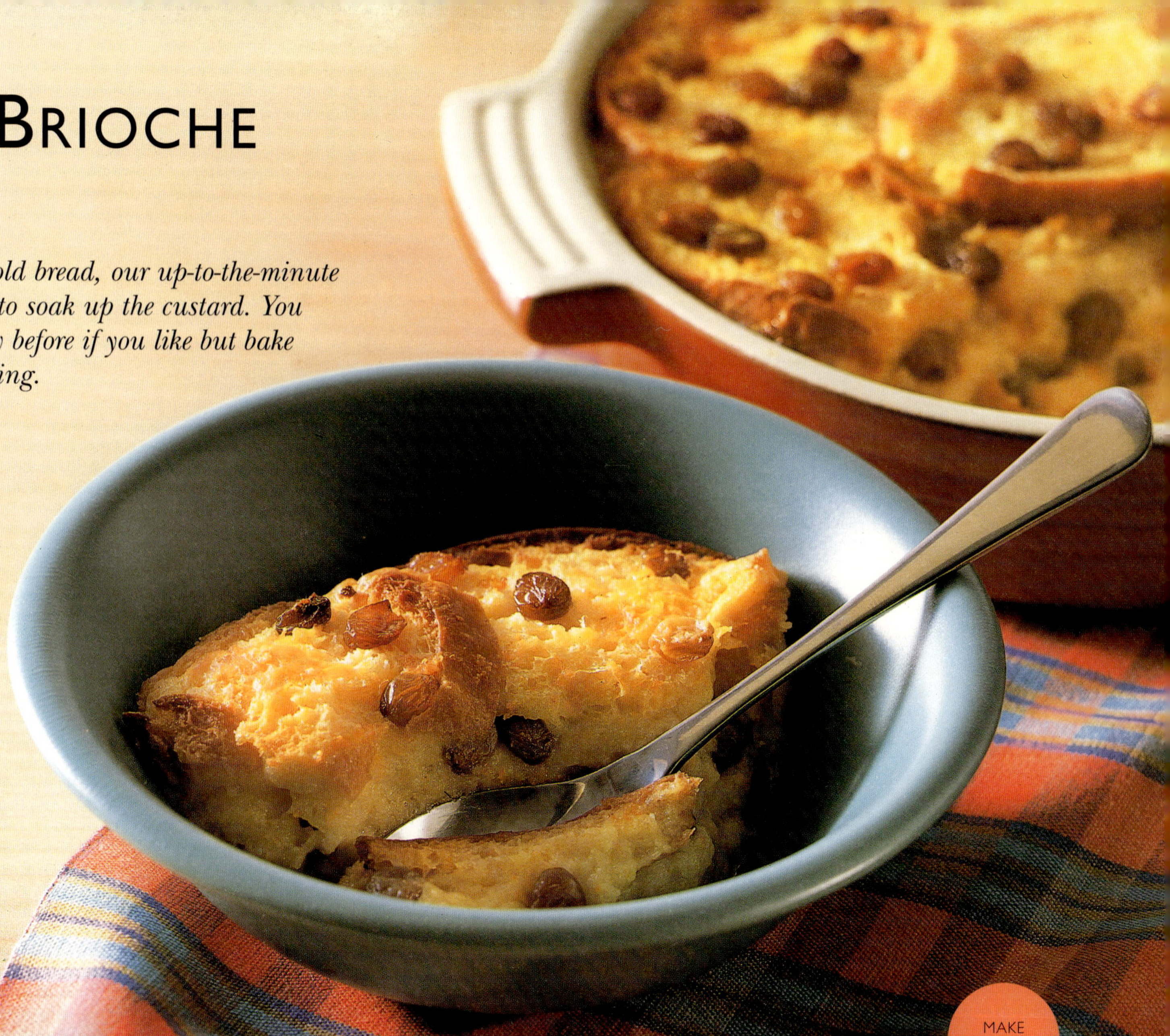

INGREDIENTS

SERVES 4–6

1 large orange
75g sultanas
4 brioche buns
25g butter, at room temperature
425g can custard
300ml milk
3 level tbsp apricot jam

MAKE AHEAD

EQUIPMENT • GRATER • KITCHEN PAPER • ROUND-BLADED KNIFE • MEDIUM BOWL • SMALL SHARP KNIFE • CUTTING BOARD • LEMON SQUEEZER • TABLESPOON • SMALL BOWL • 1.1 LITRE SHALLOW OVENPROOF DISH • CAN OPENER • FORK • BAKING SHEET

1 Grate the rind from 1 large orange being careful not to include any white pith (see page 76), and put in a medium bowl. Cut the orange in half and squeeze out the juice. Add to the bowl with 75g sultanas. Stir well and leave to marinate until required.

2 Hold each brioche bun upright on the cutting board. Cut each into 1cm thick slices.

3 With 25g softened butter, lightly butter one side of each brioche slice being careful not to drag the bread.

4 Place **one third** of the brioche bun slices over the base of a 1.1 litre dish, butter side up. Spoon **one third** of the sultana and juice mixture over the brioche slices.

5 Cover the sultanas with **half** the remaining brioche slices. Spoon **half** the remaining sultana mixture over the top. Repeat with the remaining brioche slices and sultana mixture.

6 Put the contents of a 425g can custard, 300ml milk and 3 tbsp apricot jam in the medium bowl. Whisk with a fork until well mixed, then pour over the pudding. Push the bread down with the back of the spoon and leave to soak for 1 hour. Stand the dish on a baking sheet and bake in a preheated oven at 180°C (350°F) mark 4 for 25–30 mins.

83

BUTTERED BRIOCHE PUDDING (per serving)
• CALORIES 455 • PROTEIN 10g • CARBOHYDRATE 64g
• FAT 19g • CHOLESTEROL 100mg • SODIUM 304mg

PANCAKES

Freshly cooked pancakes can be folded in half and served simply with caster sugar and lemon. Or they can be rolled over a filling and baked or cooked with a sauce.

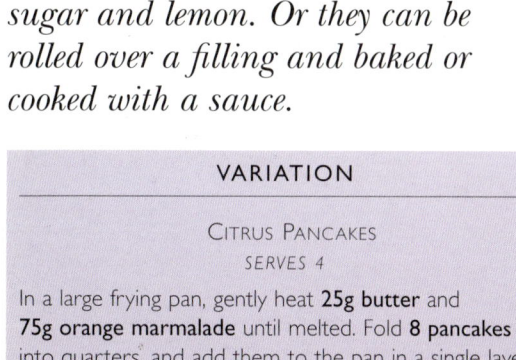

VARIATION

CITRUS PANCAKES
SERVES 4

In a large frying pan, gently heat **25g butter** and **75g orange marmalade** until melted. Fold **8 pancakes** into quarters, and add them to the pan in a single layer. Pour **150ml orange juice** and **50ml lemon juice** over and bring to the boil. Reduce the heat and simmer gently for 4–5 mins, spooning the sauce over occasionally. Serve with **caster sugar** for dredging.

BANOFFEE PANCAKES
SERVES 4

Grate **125g milk chocolate** on a coarse grater. Peel **2 large bananas**, cut them in half across, then in half lengthwise. Place one piece of banana and some grated chocolate into the centre of **8 pancakes** and drizzle a little **ready made toffee sauce** over. Fold in the sides of each pancake, then roll to enclose the filling. Grease a 1.7 litre ovenproof dish and arrange the pancakes seam side down in a single layer. Cover with foil and bake in a preheated oven at 180°C (350°F) mark 4 for about 35 mins. Serve with **cream** and extra toffee sauce.

INGREDIENTS
MAKES 8/SERVES 4

125g plain flour
¼ level tsp salt
1 egg, medium
300ml milk
about 3 tbsp vegetable oil for frying
lemon wedges to decorate
caster sugar to dredge

Pancakes (right) are traditional fare for Shrove Tuesday, but a treat any day of the year. Serve with lemon and caster sugar.

Citrus pancakes (top) are folded into quarters and simmered with butter and marmalade to make a sweet sauce.

Banoffee pancakes (left) are surprise parcels, filled with chocolate and banana, and topped with toffee sauce.

EQUIPMENT • SIEVE • MEDIUM BOWL • WOODEN SPOON • MEASURING JUG • 18CM OMELETTE PAN OR FRYING PAN • SMALL BOWL • LARGE PALETTE KNIFE

1 Sift 125g flour and ¼ tsp salt into a medium bowl. Make a well in the centre with a wooden spoon and break 1 egg into it; add **a little** of the 300ml milk. Beat the egg, gradually drawing in flour from around the sides.

2 Slowly add remaining milk, beating continuously, until the batter is smooth. Pour the batter back into the jug, cover and let stand for 10 mins.

3 Heat 3 tbsp oil in an 18cm omelette pan or frying pan. Pour off the excess into a small bowl so that just a thin coating remains in the pan.

4 Pour about **3 tbsp** of batter into the centre of the pan and immediately tilt and swirl the pan so that the batter runs over the base to give a thin layer.

5 Return pan to the heat and cook for about 1 min. When small bubbles appear in the centre of the pancake, slide a large palette knife underneath and flip over. Cook the second side for about 30 secs.

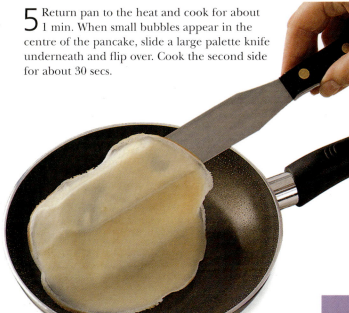

6 Slide the pancake onto a plate, fold in half, and serve with lemon wedges and a dusting of caster sugar. Eat while still warm. Reheat the pan, grease again and repeat until all the batter is used.

COOKING KNOW-HOW

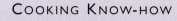

How to Stack Pancakes

If making Citrus or Banoffee Pancakes, slide the first pancake onto a piece of greaseproof paper. Stack the pancakes with a piece of greaseproof paper between each one while you finish cooking the remaining batter.

85

PANCAKES (per serving)
• CALORIES 273 • PROTEIN 7g • CARBOHYDRATE 34g
• FAT 13g • CHOLESTEROL 59mg • SODIUM 182mg

PEAR SCONE

Instead of individual cakes, serve one giant scone in wedges with butter curls and your favourite preserve. To make more traditional scones, flatten the dough to about 1cm thick and use a fluted 5cm pastry cutter to cut out small rounds. Bake 15 minutes and split when warm. Serve spread with butter or cream cheese.

SERVING TIP
To make butter curls, you can buy a small tool called a butter curler. Drag the curved blade lengthwise over a large piece of chilled butter to make the curls; chill them until ready to use.

INGREDIENTS
SERVES 4–6
225g self-raising flour

¼ level tsp salt

50g butter, at room temperature

50g soft light brown sugar

¼ level tsp ground cinnamon

½ level tsp mixed spice

2 pears

milk

TEA TIME TREAT

EQUIPMENT • LARGE BOWL • ROUND-BLADED KNIFE • CUTTING BOARD • SMALL SHARP KNIFE • GRATER • TABLESPOON • BAKING SHEET • SMALL BOWL • PASTRY BRUSH • LARGE SHARP KNIFE • WIRE COOLING RACK

1 Put 225g self-raising flour and ¼ tsp salt in a large bowl. Cut 50g butter into 4 pieces and rub into the flour using your thumb and fingertips. Stir 50g soft light brown sugar, ¼ tsp ground cinnamon, and ½ tsp mixed spice into the flour mixture then set aside until required.

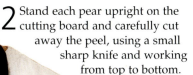

2 Stand each pear upright on the cutting board and carefully cut away the peel, using a small sharp knife and working from top to bottom.

3 Coarsely grate the pear flesh on the largest teeth of the grater, turning the pear as you reach the core until all the flesh is removed. Discard the core.

87

4 Stir grated pear into flour mixture to make a soft but not wet dough, adding about 2 tbsp milk if necessary. (If pear is very juicy, you may not need to add milk.) Form the dough into a ball with your hand.

5 Turn out the dough onto a lightly floured counter and gently shape the dough into a smooth round with your hands. Turn the dough over and flatten into a circle about 18cm in diameter using the palm of your hand. Flour your hand to prevent it sticking to the dough.

6 Lightly grease a baking sheet; transfer the scone onto it and brush the top with about 1 tbsp milk. Score into 6 wedges by cutting into the dough about 5mm with a large sharp knife. Bake in a preheated oven at 200°C (400°F) mark 6 for about 20 mins or until golden. Transfer to a wire rack to cool.

PEAR SCONE (per serving)
• CALORIES 354 • PROTEIN 6g • CARBOHYDRATE 62g
• FAT 11g • CHOLESTEROL 30mg • SODIUM 424mg

QUICK CARROT CAKE

Carrot cake is a popular tea-time or coffee break snack as well as being full of healthy ingredients. The grated carrots keep the cake moist and add texture. Using wholemeal flour adds a nutty flavour and even more goodness.

SERVING TIP

The orange flavoured cream cheese topping adds a cool contrast to the cake. Sprinkle the soft light brown sugar over the Carrot Cake just before serving.

INGREDIENTS

SERVES 4

75g wholemeal self-raising flour	50g sultanas
½ level tsp baking powder	2 eggs, medium
½ level tsp ground ginger	3 tbsp orange juice
1 level tsp ground allspice	75g soft margarine
2 carrots	150g cream cheese
75g soft light brown sugar	soft light brown sugar to dredge

COOKING KNOW-HOW

How to Line a Cake Tin with Greaseproof Paper

Stand the cake tin on top of a piece of greaseproof paper. Hold the tin steady with one hand while you trace around the base using a pencil.

Cut out the shape just inside the line, using kitchen scissors. This allows for the thickness of the tin. Grease the tin then fit the paper inside, pressing it firmly to the base. Grease the top of the greaseproof paper.

TEA-TIME SNACK OR DESSERT

EQUIPMENT • 20.5CM BASE MEASUREMENT, ROUND SANDWICH TIN • GREASEPROOF PAPER • SIEVE • LARGE BOWL • VEGETABLE PEELER • SMALL SHARP KNIFE • CUTTING BOARD • GRATER • WOODEN SPOON • BAKING SHEET • SMALL PALETTE KNIFE • WIRE COOLING RACK • MEDIUM BOWL

QUICK CARROT CAKE (per serving)
• CALORIES 533 • PROTEIN 8g • CARBOHYDRATE 47g
• FAT 36g • CHOLESTEROL 133mg • SODIUM 386mg

1 Grease and line a 20.5cm round sandwich tin (see pages 7 and 88). Sieve 75g self-raising flour, ½ tsp baking powder, ½ tsp ginger and 1 tsp allspice into a large bowl. Add wheat flakes from sieve to bowl.

2 Peel 2 carrots, trim the ends and cut in half across the middle. Coarsely grate each piece on the largest teeth of the grater. Add to the bowl with 75g soft light brown sugar and 50g sultanas.

3 Add 2 eggs, **1 tbsp** orange juice and 75g margarine to the bowl; stand it on a damp cloth to steady it. Beat the mixture well using a wooden spoon until the ingredients are well combined and the mixture is soft.

4 Stand the prepared tin on on a baking sheet, pour in the cake mixture and level the surface using a small palette knife. Bake in a preheated oven at 190°C (375°F) mark 5 for 20–25 mins or until well risen and a toothpick inserted into the centre comes out clean. Allow to stand in the tin for 10 mins.

5 Run the palette knife or a round-bladed knife around the sides of the cake to loosen it from the tin. Carefully tip the warm cake onto your hand and peel away the lining paper. Place the wire rack on the base of the cake then tip the cake back onto the rack to cool.

6 In a medium bowl beat together 150g cream cheese and remaining 2 tbsp of orange juice using a wooden spoon. Spread over the top of the cooled cake. Transfer the cake to a plate and sprinkle over a little soft brown sugar before serving.

VARIATION ON A CLASSIC

LEMON SHORTBREAD FINGERS

Traditional Scottish shortbread is given a zesty flavour with added lemon. Cut into fingers, as shown here, or squares if you prefer, while the shortbread is still warm from the oven.

SERVING TIP As well as being a traditional tea time biscuit, these shortbread fingers would be an excellent accompaniment to summer fruits and ice cream.

INGREDIENTS
....
MAKES 24

175g butter at room temperature
1 lemon
75g caster sugar
175g plain flour
50g ground rice
caster sugar to dredge

INGREDIENT NOTE
Ground rice is the traditional ingredient used to give shortbread its fine texture. It can be found in the supermarket or health food stores alongside the rice products, and is available fine, medium or coarse ground. Fine is the most commonly used and is the one needed for this recipe.

06

2 Grate rind from 1 lemon being careful not to include any white pith (see page 76). Add 75g caster sugar and lemon rind to the butter and beat until it is pale and fluffy.

1 Grease a 20.5 cm base measurement, square deep cake tin (see page 7). Put 175g butter in a medium bowl; stand bowl on a damp cloth to steady it. Beat the butter until soft, using a wooden spoon.

3 Add 175g plain flour and 50g ground rice and stir using the wooden spoon, until the ingredients begin to stick together.

4 Tip mixture into the prepared tin, and press it into an even layer over the base of the tin, using floured fingers.

6 Let the shortbread stand for 10 mins then cut into fingers using a round-bladed knife. Let cool completely in the tin. Dredge with caster sugar before serving.

5 Prick the dough all over with a fork making sure the prongs go right through to the tin. Bake in a preheated oven at 170°C (325°F) mark 3 for 20–25 mins or until pale golden brown.

LEMON SHORTBREAD FINGERS (per serving)
• CALORIES 99 • PROTEIN 1g • CARBOHYDRATE 11g
• FAT 6g • CHOLESTEROL 17mg • SODIUM 55mg

STICKY CHOCOLATE BROWNIES

These brownies really do stand up to their name – the stickiness is part of their appeal. This is a recipe borrowed from America and it is at home with coffee, tea or as a dessert. A word of warning, do not make these for calorie conscious guests. The temptation will be just too great to resist.

SERVING TIP As well as serving at tea time, turn these brownies into a dessert by serving them with a scoop of ice cream.

92

INGREDIENTS

MAKES ABOUT 16 SQUARES

225g white chocolate
350g plain chocolate
225g butter
3 eggs, medium
3 level tbsp runny honey
225g soft light brown sugar
75g self-raising flour
¼ level tsp salt
175g walnut pieces

MAKING A MEAL

When planning your menus, keep in mind the flavours of the different courses. If you plan to serve a spicy main course, such as Chilli con Carne or Thai Chicken Curry, choose a refreshing dessert. If your menu has a light main course, like Pan-Fried Salmon, a more robust dessert, like Plum Nut Tart, would provide a good choice. In addition, here are some quick and easy ways to add to a meal.

SIMPLE STARTERS
- Serve ready-made taramasalata or hummus with hot toast or pitta bread and bowls of olives.
- Serve prepared dips with crisps, or pieces of cucumber and carrot.
- Select four or five different salamis and hams, arrange on a platter and serve with ready-made potato salad, cherry tomatoes and gherkins.

- Serve wedges of juicy ripe melon drizzled with a little liqueur or served with wafer thin slices of prosciutto.
- Toss cooked peeled prawns and diced avocado in a little Classic French or Creamy Lemon Dressing (see page 71).
- Bake a selection of breaded seafood pieces, such as sole goujons and scampi, and serve with tartare sauce and lemon wedges.

ADD SOME VEGETABLES
A little cooking know how is all that is needed when cooking fresh vegetables (see page 68); follow these times as a guide:
- Peas, mangetout, sugarsnap peas: simmer for 3–5 mins.
- Sprouts, broccoli, cauliflower, cabbage, courgettes, green beans: simmer for 5–10 mins.
- Root vegetables, such as potatoes, carrots, parsnips, celeriac: simmer for 15–20 mins.

EASY ENDINGS
- Marinate fresh fruit in a little of your favourite liqueur and serve with scoops of ice cream.
- Pour sparkling white wine over red summer berries just before serving.

- Heat bakery-made Danish pastries or muffins in the oven and serve with lashings of cream.
- Slice your favourite fruit and place in a heatproof dish, dot with spoonfuls of mascarpone cheese, and sprinkle some brown sugar over. Grill under a hot grill until the sugar melts, the cheese is bubbling and the fruit warmed through.
- Mix together strong coffee, a little sugar, and coffee liqueur to taste, and freeze in a container overnight. Mash with a fork to break up into crystals and freeze again until required. Serve with whipped cream.
- Offer a cheese board at the end of the meal. For the best flavour, serve the cheese at room temperature, taking it out of the refrigerator at least 2 hours before you wish to eat it. Serve a selection of different cheeses, about 3 or 4 – a good combination would be a blue cheese such as Stilton or Gorgonzola, a creamy goat's cheese or Camembert and a hard cheese like Lancashire or Cheddar or a semi-hard variety like Jarlsberg or Emmenthal. Along with biscuits, serve some grapes, apple quarters or celery sticks on the cheese board.

INDEX